To Christine

Joe

EMPRESS EUGENIE

A footnote history
1826-1920

Joanne Watson

Grosvenor House
Publishing Limited

This book is published by
Grosvenor House Publishing Ltd
Link House
140 The Broadway, Tolworth, Surrey, KT6 7HT.
www.grosvenorhousepublishing.co.uk

A CIP record for this book
is available from the British Library

ISBN 978-1-83975-993-2

Introduction

Imagine an International celebrity at the centre of a huge empire, a fashion icon, proto feminist, "guardian angel" of the Suez Canal, friend of Queen Victoria, forced to make a daring escape to avoid death at the hands of a mob. Eugenie lived in exile in England for 50 years, most as a widow with 4 decades spent in a small Hampshire town having lost her only child fighting for a British cause.

Whilst Eugenie's Imperial life in France during the glamorous Second Empire was recorded in newspapers worldwide, gossiped about endlessly, she steadfastly refused to have her life and times recorded officially and destroyed hundreds of private documents.

Reading the serious histories of her life I found the asides and footnotes so intriguing it drew me to explore them further. The increased digitalisation made many new and interesting sources available and provided several exciting discoveries.

What I write is a mixture of facts, observations of her contemporaries all drawn from the numerous reports and versions of her life and times. Whilst I don't ignore the main historical landmarks and there is some logical supposition in the narrative, her life was captivating enough to require little invention as she said herself "Never waste time dramatising life".

Contents

List of illustrations

Chapter One

The Early Years

Eugenie c1853. Marie-Pauline Laurent.
Metropolitan Museum Public Domain

Eugenie or María Eugenia Ignacia Agustina de Palafox-Portocarrero de Guzman y Kirkpatrick was born on May 5th 1826 in Granada, Spain in the middle of an earthquake. Her birth in a makeshift tent in the garden of the family home was certainly unusual, quakes were fairly frequent in the area but it would have been frightening none the less and according to any local fortune teller inauspicious.

Her mother Maria Manuela was half Scottish, a quarter Belgian and a quarter Spanish, the daughter of a wealthy expat Scottish wine merchant who doubled up as an honorary American consul and a Belgian mother. Eugenie's father was a soldier and aristocrat, Don Cipriano de Palafox y Portocarrero. He'd had a distinguished military career and was nine years older than his wife, a striking fellow with a full head of red hair and black eye patch, the consequence of losing an eye whilst fighting for the Napoleonic side in the Peninsular Wars. His battlefield endeavours earned him the Legion d'honneur from the French but disfavour amongst many countrymen. He was also the second son of a major grandee but his brother had no children and little prospect of producing an heir so for the social climber that Maria had become, an obvious target. Both were Bonapartists but totally opposite in temperament.

They had two daughters, Maria, known as Paca and Eugenie. Some expressed doubts as to who had actually fathered Eugenie as the likely date of conception they argued, coincided with his time in jail because of his Napoleonic allegiances. There was even a suggestion she was really the child of a liaison with a future British Foreign Secretary, Lord Clarendon. Her mother's reply…the dates don't match!

Eugenie's childhood was relatively spartan, a result of her father's jail terms which drained the family coffers. She and her elder sister, Paca, were made to walk wherever possible, the horses they rode were often shoeless and Eugenie would regularly ride bareback her auburn hair flowing behind, sometimes it was said whilst smoking a cigar. She adored bullfights where she would dress and flirt outrageously, which didn't go unnoticed. She had a lifetime love of the outdoors, though one risky outing was nearly fatal as she had to be saved from drowning. Headstrong and impetuous, all in all not your typical Empressorial CV.

The family lifestyle improved significantly when her uncle died in 1834 and her father inherited the titles, all 18 of them. They moved to Madrid but the same year fled the city because of a cholera outbreak and a neighbourhood riot during a period of civil unrest and spent a couple of years in Paris. Eugenie's school report from the progressive "Gymnase Normal, Civil et Orthosomatique", for 1836 to 1837 praised her strong liking for athletic exercise and although an indifferent student, her character was "good, generous, active and firm".

The sisters were then packed off to boarding school in Clifton in Bristol to learn English but the regime didn't appeal to the 11 year old Eugenie. She was repeatedly teased and called "carrots" because of her hair and went as far as launching an escape bid. Along with two young Indian princesses who felt equally oppressed they managed to sneak onto a boat in Bristol in a bid for freedom but the scheme was foiled by Paca who spilled the beans on their plans. It did have the desired outcome as they left Britain and were ultimately sent back to Paris where they were largely home schooled under the watchful eyes of two English governesses. One of her mother's friends based in Paris was Prosper Mérimée, the author of the book on which the opera Carmen was based. Some suggest it drew on stories told by Maria and he was to serve as a useful informer on Parisian society and confidante to Eugenie in the years ahead.

Their stay in the capital was halted when their father died in 1839 and they returned to Madrid to finish their education. Her mother, a lively outgoing person and acknowledged beauty was risqué by most standards but was now part of the wider Spanish royal circle and their aristocratic system was and still is a magnet for titles. Since some could be passed down the female line there were certainly a few to spare and enough for Eugenie to become Eugenie de Montijo, Countess of Teba.

By now she had grown into a beautiful young woman and fallen in love. One intense attachment was to the son of the Duke of Alba, one of the richest men in Europe, but he went on to marry her sister Paca. That hit Eugenie hard. Another potential suitor who'd been romancing her turned out he'd been using her as a way to meet her sister. When it became clear he wasn't serious, Eugenie took a concoction of phosphorus (match heads) and milk in a suicide attempt. Only when he arrived, not to comfort her but to take back his letters did she realise the hopelessness of her case and take a hermetic but it left her seriously ill for several weeks.

How many other matches were discussed or proposals received isn't clear but Maria Manuela was now a society hostess and several suitable suitors buzzed around Eugenie. Whilst she was happy to flirt with them none appealed, or those she was interested in didn't reciprocate her feelings and she earned the reputation of being a bit of a tease. She was taken on visits to London and Paris but despite her looks and titles no acceptable marriage proposals were forthcoming but in 1849 she met her future husband, Louis Napoleon. The occasion was a lavish reception at the Elysee Palace as Napoleon was now the President of the Second Republic and he was certainly interested in her. "What is the road to your heart?" Napoleon inquired, "through the chapel, Sire", she answered. She'd been well briefed on his dubious reputation but his interest spurred on her ambitious mother. If her elder daughter had married a Duke, could the younger one fare even better. Eugenie was 23 and no longer in the first flush of debutante youth and it must have been something of a long shot.

Louis Napoleon 1852 Le Gray
Met Museum PD

(Charles) Louis Napoleon was the third son of Napoleon Bonaparte's brother Louis and the daughter of Empress Josephine by her first marriage, Hortense de Beauharnais. Even his paternal parentage is disputed, his father periodically denied it and he bore little physical resemblance to his famous uncle.

He did though have similar undisguised ambitions which resulted in periods of exile and imprisonment.

Born in Paris but exiled after Waterloo he lived in Switzerland, briefly in Italy and was schooled in Bavaria which left its mark with a german twang to his accent. For much of his twenties he was in England with his mother but gradually as the more senior heirs to the Bonaparte dynasty, including Napoleon II, son of the great Emperor died off, Louis Napoleon became the prime figurehead for a return to Bonaparte rule.

His first attempt at seizing power in 1836 was an abject failure, he certainly wasn't a heroic figure, which is perhaps why instead of jail he was sent on a very slow boat to exile in New York. The 4 month voyage took them via Rio de Janeiro, definitely not the most direct route but whether he would have settled in the US was never determined as a few months later he was on a speedier boat back across the Atlantic to England. His mother was seriously ill and with a borrowed American passport he made a furtive visit to her in Switzerland. Her death a couple of months later brought him enough money to set himself up in style back in London. Imperial eagles on his carriage, (followed it was said by a small tiger on occasion) he wore Savile row suits and a diamond studded cravat which along with his moustache and goatee beard made him a conspicuous fellow. The invitations from the great and the good, both political and social soon followed. He occasionally ventured out of the capital with regular jaunts to join the county hunting set but perhaps as significant was a visit to Southport. It's claimed the main avenue, Lord Street, was the inspiration for the now familiar tree lined boulevards developed in Paris a few decades later.

Whilst not physically attractive, with a long trunk, short legs and slightly waddling gait, Louis Napoleon looked much better on horseback than in the society drawing rooms, but he had charisma, charm and a twinkling eye. No wonder distrusting society mothers kept a keen lookout for their unsuspecting daughters. His name appealed or was feared depending on which side of the channel you stood.

Behind this gentlemanly façade Louis Napoleon was plotting his next course of action but an attempted coup in 1840 started inauspiciously via a hired tourist steamer to Boulogne and was equally underwhelming. He made it to Paris but under armed escort and this time the punishment was perpetual imprisonment in the imposing fortress of Ham, in northern France. It had seen service as guardians of other famous prisoners including Joan of Arc and was a grim prison with damp walls and the feel of unrelenting melancholy. It did little for his health and might have been the end of his dynastic dreams. Somehow he managed to persuade the authorities to loosen their ties and be allowed certain privileges. Amongst them were a steady supply of books which he read voraciously and enabled him to write several pamphlets to further his cause. Equally but perhaps more unusually he was allowed female company which came in the form of a voluptuous young servant nicknamed "La Belle Sabotiere". Their liaisons produced two children and he would later provide her with an apartment in the Champs-Élysées, however her homely comforts weren't enough to keep him happy and after more than 5 years he forced his escape. On May 25th 1846 with some outside help from his former conspirators he was disguised as one of the many workmen employed at the fortress. Aided perhaps by the familiar dummy in the bed tactic to delay discovery he walked out carrying a plank of wood and made a swift return to London, arrived at a society party and gave a French attaché the fright of his life. (When Napoleon became Emperor he appointed the Governor of Ham to the same role at St Cloud).

Prison had aged Napoleon significantly and he needed time to recover his health.

The British Government allowed Louis to stay but quite why they were so sanguine about his presence is unclear since it was very evident what his intentions were given even half a chance. Buoyed by an inheritance from his father which replenished his coffers he set about a period of rehabilitation, spending time in the country and building up his strength. His renewed vigour was apparent to the Ladies too, though his reputed conquests were on such a scale that even Don Giovanni would have found impossible to attain. If women were an attraction, they were never a distraction to his ultimate aim and he was prepared to wait a little longer.

France meanwhile was a country still trying to decide what sort of government it really wanted which resulted in repeated periods of unrest. This came to a head in that year of revolutions, 1848 when in February the ageing King Louis Philippe was ousted and escaped to exile in Britain. Louis Napoleon on hearing the news is said to have jumped out of his bath and headed the other way but his stay in Paris was short lived and almost immediately he was back to London biding his time until the inevitable turmoil subsided. Strangely a few months later he was enrolled as a Special Constable dealing with the Chartist riots in the capital. Louis had little active political experience but the Bonaparte name carried him a long way and when it was announced there'd be elections, he put his name forward and was elected in absentia. Under threat of imprisonment, he stayed away but his next successful election attempt was rewarded with the longed for return to Paris along with a wealthy mistress Lizzie Howard. Despite a less than impressive presence in the chamber, he had a meteoric rise becoming Prince President in 1848 but with his term nearing an end and so many opposing factions he staged a swiftly executed and bloody Coup d'etat in December 1851. It was followed by a referendum of dubious integrity a year later with an unlikely 97% vote in favour. He emerged as Emperor Napoleon lll and a new, bright, glamorous but repressive Second Empire was born. Few who knew him in Britain could have anticipated such a rise to power. His stay in London was recognised a few years later by a Blue Plaque, the only one awarded to a living person.

Napoleon's new status brought dynastic ambitions and the need of a wife. He was tempted by Eugenie, the Montijos were regular guests at receptions and parties but not content to pursue her alone he looked for a bride amongst several royal houses. These included 16 year old Princess Adelaide, a niece of Queen Victoria's but religion, reputation and family disquiet, especially from Victoria and Albert sank that match and he fared no better amongst other royal candidates. Few thought his long term prospects any good and most regarded him as an upstart.

Whilst Napoleon cast his net around Europe, Eugenie was in an invidious position, she waited, saw the speculation and was faced with a court most of whom looked down their noses at her. His ministers advised against the match and large bets were gambled on the outcome with several courtiers backing a royal alliance. Napoleon seemingly besotted, proposed and Eugenie accepted though not without some qualms, as she outlined in a letter to her sister "on the eve of mounting one of the greatest thrones of Europe, I cannot help feeling somewhat terrified". She was 26 and he was 44. Those who had wagered otherwise lost quite heavily, even the Bourse, the French stock exchange, hiccupped violently.

The engagement in January 1853 was met with a lukewarm response in France despite his forthright stance "I have preferred a woman whom I love and respect to a woman unknown to me, with whom an alliance would have had advantages mixed with sacrifices". Many thought it a come down despite her title and if the new Empress wasn't going to be a royal Princess then the nation thought he could have found a French bride. The foreign press were equally unimpressed, The Times was quite scathing. "We learn with some amusement that this romantic event in the annals of the French Empire has called forth the strongest opposition, and provoked the utmost irritation. The Imperial family, the Council of Ministers, and even the lower coteries of the palace, all affect to regard this marriage as an amazing humiliation". The British Ambassador, Lord Cowley summed it up succinctly "She has played her game so well that he can get her in no other way but marriage".

The gap between engagement and the wedding was just a week, perhaps because none of the foreign dignitaries were the least bit interested in attending. The bride and her mother were installed at the Élysées Palace and the civil service took place in the Tuileries on the evening of January 29th 1853.

Musée Carnavalet CCØ

The marriage wasn't official until the church service the following day at Notre Dame.

Eugenie was about five foot five, pale skinned with blue violet eyes and much admired auburn hair, a Titianesque beauty. She made a striking impression, a graceful young woman, a modern day trophy wife perhaps. Dressed in a long white velvet gown bejewelled and decorated with old English lace and orange blossom Eugenie's diadem coronet was decorated with diamonds and sapphires from the royal collection, previously worn at Empress Josephine's coronation. To this she'd added her own pearls wrapped in four rows round her neck. One outspoken Spanish woman in the crowd quoted an old Castilian saying which foretold misery for any bride who chose those Jewels. "The pearls that women wear on their wedding day represent the tears that they are feted to shed".

Napoleon, his trademark moustache waxed and turned up at the edges was resplendent in a scarlet jacket, gold epaulettes, ribbons and medals of various orders. The Imperial pomp ensured a fitting, if over long ceremony, with thousands of candles illuminating the proceedings. The crowds turned up more out of curiosity than support as the fledgling Empire was still not secure.

After an intimate private lunch Eugenie might have hoped for a quiet start to their honeymoon but the plans had been left in the hands of his cousin Princess Mathilde who had a different agenda so they found themselves unexpectedly lumbered with a lavish civil reception. They were then left waiting on the doorstep for a carriage to take them to their apartments in the grounds of St Cloud.

If outsiders expected the Empress to have the life of a fairytale Princess they would be mistaken though Eugenie did fare better than her two contemporary Imperial spouses. Elizabeth "Sisi" who married the Austrian Emperor Franz Joseph in 1854 buckled under the pressure of public scrutiny, court snobbery, family tragedy and estrangement and was assassinated in 1898. Her sister-in-law, Charlotte, a Belgian princess married Franz Joseph's younger brother Maximilian in 1857. They were persuaded by Napoleon to rule the ill fated and short-lived Mexican Empire. When the government collapsed Maximilian was executed by firing squad and Charlotte suffered a severe mental breakdown and spent her final years hidden away.

Chapter Two

Married Life

On becoming President, Napoleon had settled himself in the Tuileries, "place for manufacturing tiles". The Palace bordered the Seine, and was a leisurely 30 minute walk to Notre Dame.

Paris Panorama 1850. Tuileries in the foreground, Louvre behind it.
Rue de Rivoli to the left and Notre Dame in the Island in the River Seine.
Charles Fichot. Library of Congress (LOC)

Not always the favoured residence of previous rulers it had suffered from the neglect of generations and damage from the riots of 1848 so necessitated substantial repairs and restoration. This was done to reflect the Bonaparte family, the hangings and upholstery were in green, the family colour, and portraits and busts of Bonaparte's generals were positioned in the significant areas, such as the Salle des Maréchaux, the imposing hall of the generals.

Salle des Maréchaux . 1852. Musée Carnavalet 1852 CCØ

There was an abundance of gold, gilt and crystal but an absence of running water and heating in large parts of the palace and walking through the warren of gloomy, narrow, gas lit, unventilated passages was an unpleasant experience.

The Empress had ten apartments on the first floor, including three colour coded rooms, pink, blue and green salons and a winding staircase linked these to the Emperor's rooms on the ground floor. She looked out onto the elegant gardens, down the flower bordered, tree lined Champs-Élysées towards The Arc de Triomphe. There were three other main palaces, St Cloud to the west of the city their base in the Spring, Fontainebleau to the south in the early summer and good for hunting and Compiègne in the north east, the venue for a series of lavish autumn parties.

The hill top Chateau of St Cloud, overlooking Paris was Eugenie's favourite, it had more than 600 rooms and was renowned for its beautiful gardens and famed water fountains. It had been bought by Louis XVI for his wife Marie Antoinette. The "Martyr Queen" had gone to the guillotine in 1793 but much of that era, pre-Revolution was now fashionable. She too was a foreigner, an Austrian, an outsider and that resonated with Eugenie who developed a near obsession with the former Queen. Within a short walk from the Palace through a pleasant park was a small country-house called "Villeneuve l'Etang," which the Emperor had given to Eugenie and where they'd spent their wedding night. Here she could enjoy playing at being Marie Antoinette, there was a Swiss dairy in imitation of the Queen's and the gardens had the feel of the Petit Trianon at Versailles. Eugenie began to gather furniture and paintings from the period to decorate the Palaces and collected numerous pieces of memorabilia such as a scrapbook of fabrics from her wardrobes and snuff boxes. Into the mix she added important contemporary furniture and decorations, the result was a standard of luxury that existed beyond the fall of the Empire and was adopted by many a 5 star hotel in the period up to the First World War.

The cost of the renovations and refurbishments of the Royal Palaces was extensive and coupled with the substantial expenditure of running the Imperial households combined to create a major financial burden. Napoleon wasn't regarded as personally extravagant but he'd been generous to his supporters and had debts in England to add to a growing bill.

From the beginning Eugenie was keenly aware of the disquiet amongst some of the French and acted with caution and pragmatism in trying to win over the critics. The City of Paris had offered her a diamond valued at the time at £24,000 instead she asked for that sum to be used for the establishment of a school for young girls of a poor background. Another gift of £10,000 from the Emperor was distributed to a variety of charitable causes. It mollified many but Eugenie's Spanish heritage would always be used against her in times of crisis. As for her mother, she was given her marching orders by Napoleon early in their marriage and encouraged not to return too often.

It's now worth considering the other leading Bonapartists, at best you could describe them as ungrateful, Napoleon's elevation had brought them major benefits not least financial but there was considerable underlying and barely disguised jealousy.

The head of the other branch was the ageing Prince Jerome but it was his son Napoleon (Joseph) who figured quite largely. He was known by most by his peculiar nickname of Plon Plon, due to his childhood difficulties in pronouncing his own name. Given the Princely title by Napoleon when he became President, he was the second son of Bonaparte's younger brother Jerome by his second marriage.

He fancied himself as a general and served in the Crimean and Italian Wars but had little military aptitude. He kept such a low profile, that after his absence at the Battle of Solferino his troops called him "Craint-Plomb" (Afraid of Lead). He bore a striking resemblance to the great Bonaparte and whilst intelligent was personally coarse, rude and generally despised, even Queen Victoria, who only met him occasionally called him disagreeable. Many years later the young Prince Imperial (the heir to the throne) asked his father what the difference was between an accident and misfortune. The Emperor replied with as much

Prince Napoleon. Musée Carnavalet CCØ

gravity as he could manage "Well, if our cousin Napoleon were to fall into the Seine, it would be an 'accident.' If someone pulled him out, it would be a misfortune"!

Whilst he was an advisor to the Emperor, Plon Plon held firm anti clerical views which clashed with the Catholicism of the Empress. He was reputed to deliberately eat meat on a Friday which went against Catholic practice and on one occasion when the Emperor asked him to propose a toast to the Empress on her birthday, he flatly refused.

His sister was Princess Mathilde who'd been engaged to the Emperor before his imprisonment in Ham. She subsequently married a rich Russian nobleman but it was a stormy relationship and after they split up she lived in a mansion in Paris and acted as hostess for Napoleon when he was single.

Mathilde was a cultured woman, schooled in the arts and became an important patron during the Second Empire, as well as hosting an influential salon. These gatherings regularly attracted around 100 people including major artists and literati. This was her empire and she had no apparent regrets about not having married Napoleon and politically she fell out with him on several occasions.

She'd first met Eugenie in 1845 and felt she was a "woman accustomed to homage from men". In other words, Eugenie's beauty was a given so she was pretty immune to flattery. Eugenie's attempts to establish some form of friendship got nowhere. She once

Princess Mathilde. Musée Carnavalet 1852 CCØ

15

sent her a couple of dresses but Mathilde responded by sending her a sausage which the Empress thanked her for profusely! They held completely opposite views on virtually everything and Mathilde would spread increasingly vindictive gossip lapped up by friends and foes alike.

To give you an idea about the Paris grapevine, just a few months after the wedding, Karl Marx wrote about one of Eugenie's failings in a letter to Frederick Engels. "That angel suffers, it seems, from a most indelicate complaint. She is passionately addicted to farting, and is incapable, even in company, of suppressing it. At one time she resorted to horse-riding as a remedy. But this was later forbidden (by her husband) so she now vents herself. It's only a noise, a little murmur... but then you know that the French are sensitive to the slightest puff of wind." Given that Marx was exiled in London at the time, word had spread quickly, an unenviable consequence of being at the centre of the public eye in the new Empire.

If the Imperial wedding had been a success and a great spectacle the wedding night was apparently less so, certainly from Eugenie's perspective. She was heard to remark that sex was disgusting. It was however a necessary evil as the Emperor wanted an heir. Eugenie did fall pregnant almost immediately but suffered a miscarriage and it's said Napoleon stayed faithful for six months before returning to his philandering. Her failure to carry a child to term was attributed by Napoleon to her regular horse riding and had been banned, as Marx observed.

At times Eugenie must have felt like an exotic bird in a gilded cage, much admired but with her wings clipped and no prospect of the freedom she'd enjoyed when she was single. She regarded herself as the "leading slave of the kingdom" and resented her lack of privacy. Her spontaneity was frowned on and her normal daily life, after the novelty had worn off, didn't appeal.

She got up about between 8 and 9, occupied herself in whatever appealed or was required, then ate brunch with the Emperor alone at 11.30. Her Ladies in waiting came in at 2pm and then she went on a daily carriage drive to the Bois de Boulogne with one of them, repeatedly bowing to the crowd. She came home, dressed for dinner and afterwards the assembled guests did or said, ...well very little, unless prompted by either Napoleon or Eugenie. The ladies sat in a circle, the gentleman standing behind. The Emperor had a soft languid voice but rarely spoke and it was left to the Empress to relieve the monotony with a constant stream of chatter. She spoke fluent French, but with a noticeable Spanish accent. Sarah Bernhardt, the legendary French actress was asked to reprise a role at the Tuileries and on first meeting thought the Empress more beautiful than her portraits, that was until she spoke. She described Eugenie's voice as rough, hard and ugly which rather broke the spell.

Lots of activities were tried to relieve the boredom including artificial flower making which sent the chamberlain scurrying off to find the necessary elements at 9pm. Another report mentions an indoor game called "potting the candles", kicking rubber balls at lighted candles, the aim being to knock them over and extinguish the light. Any suggestion that the "Reader" should perform her duties rarely met with any consensus as to the subject matter. Normally at 10 a tea tray would be brought in after which Napoleon would retire to "transact business with his private secretary", a euphemism quite frequently for his extra marital pleasures. Eugenie would stay up until around 1130 and whilst she had seemingly endless energy the guests were definitely wilting and only when she left could the gentleman sit down. There was a lot of standing around in royal circles. Eugenie herself would retire to her apartments and often sit up into the early hours.

In search of diversion she developed an interest in spiritualism which was popular in Paris at one time and would host seances in the Palace, regarded as scandalous in some quarters. A report in an American newspaper, the Philadelphia Times, described how on one occasion a famous Victorian medium Daniel Dunglas Home persuaded the Emperor that he'd summoned the great Bonaparte into the darkened room to shake hands with him. Home had in fact taken off his shoes and as he was only wearing a cut off sock with bare toes when he managed to swing his foot onto to the Emperor's hand he could convincingly claim this cold, clammy apparition was that of his illustrious uncle. It caused great consternation to all present.

To reinforce her status Eugenie was given some solo formal duties and held audiences with those requesting the opportunity to put their case to her or Napoleon. They were rather like a court of appeal, some came requesting justice, others wanting money and amongst them the occasional charlatan who tried to prey on her sympathetic and sincere nature. These audiences were held standing up as they felt if the petitioners were allowed to sit down, they would never get rid of them.

One of the most striking portraits of the Empress was painted as a private commission in 1853 (on the book cover). The full length portrait shows her in 18th costume, in a pale gold taffeta dress over a white petticoat, with blue ribbons, black knots and powdered hair. Set in a woodland glade, unusually the portrait shows a sideways view of Eugenie. It would hang in her private Salle de Dames in the Tuileries throughout her reign. The artist was Franz Xaver Winterhalter, a German painter who was already established for his fashionable court portraiture with patrons such as King Louis Philippe and Queen Victoria. His skill was combining the sitter's likeness with virtuosic detail of dress (his speciality) in a subtle idealised manner which made him very popular with his clientele but drew criticism from the critics. I doubt he was concerned since as his reputation spread he was the go to painter for royals and the aristocracy throughout Europe. He was unusual as he generally painted directly onto the canvas without prior sketching and aided by his numerous assistants could deliver with conveyor belt speed. Victoria commissioned more than 120 paintings from him, many family scenes on a grand scale and sometimes wanted copies of a favourite painting so she could have one version at Osborne for example and another at Windsor or Balmoral.

Perhaps the most famous of his Eugenie paintings shows her with eight of her Ladies in waiting in a pastoral setting.

Eugenie and her Ladies – Winterhalter. Musee du Château Compiegne
©2021 RMN- Grand Palais/Dist.Photo SCALA, Florence

The painting is larger than life, 3 x 4.2m and the composition is similar to one of his earlier more erotic works called Florinda. The Empress off set slightly to the left, seated above her ladies and is shown handing a bunch of violets to her most important Lady in waiting, the Grand Maitresse. There is a deliberate absence of jewellery giving more emphasis to her pale skin and bare shoulders. Although it looks like a charming gathering, the critics weren't impressed, not that they said so openly for fear of punishment. The painting was displayed initially at the World Fair in 1855 and then at the Palace of Fontainebleau but would eventually be returned to the Empress whilst in exile and hung in the foyer of her house at Farnborough Hill.

The Ladies in waiting were an important part of her life, she only knew a few of them when they were appointed but all had the appropriate social standing. Later she would add more from amongst her friends. The senior ladies, who were given the rank of "grand officier," wore a small portrait of the Empress set in diamonds, hanging from a knot of ribbon fastened on the left shoulder. The others were identified by a small gold and blue enamel brooch, edged with diamonds and the initials IE (Imperatrice Eugenie) also in diamonds in the centre and above a similarly decorated crown. The brooch was attached to a ribbon which could be pinned to a dress. All were paid appointments.

The hierarchy was a Grand-Maitresse, (Mistress of the Robes) the Princess d'Essling and her deputy, a Dame d'honneur (Matron of Honour), the Duchess of Bassano. The third person was a Demoiselle d'honneur (Maid of Honour). There were then six Dames des Palais (Ladies in waiting), later this was increased to 12 after the birth of the Prince Imperial. These would work in alternating pairs fulfilling the daily duties.

As the most Senior lady, Anne d'Essling, the Duchess of Rivoli had to supervise all the other Ladies and their schedule and review all the applications from those wishing for an audience. That sounds rather tedious and she normally delegated this to Countess Bassano. Both would be present with the Empress at all grander public and state occasions, and had to stand throughout so it could be pretty tiring. d'Essling wouldn't necessarily attend court daily except when the Empress was at the Tuileries. One essential part of her role was to review the guest lists for the major functions, given these were often extremely large gatherings it was important to ensure no important name was missed off the list or included in error. She was also a well connected society hostess, and her salon was regarded as one of the most charming and polite in Paris. She stayed with Eugenie for the duration of the Empire.

Pauline, Duchess of Bassano was married to a diplomat who became Napoleon's Chamberlain and later joined him in exile. She was an imposing figure described by a contemporary as a very distinguished looking woman with "a most charming manner who performed her duties with much discretion". She died in 1867 and was replaced by the Countess Walewska, who was one of Napoleon's mistresses. Ironically her husband was almost certainly one of the great Bonaparte's lookalike illegitimate children!

The Maid of Honour, was the primary reader. This lady was required to read to the Empress as required, however Eugenie much preferred to read herself.

One of her ordinary Ladies in waiting was an American, Jane Thorne who the Empress had known before her marriage. Eugenie would often speak to her in English to keep up her fluency. Renowned as an excellent horsewoman she would accompany the Empress out riding but she had one major failing, she smoked (which Eugenie hated) and would apparently sometimes blow smoke in her face, presumably by accident. Napoleon was a chain smoker and his study would reek of the smell. Eugenie stayed out of the room and resorted to banging a gong at the bottom of the stairs if she wished to speak to him. When asked why he didn't ban tobacco he replied. "This vice brings in one hundred million Francs in taxes every year. I will certainly forbid it at once—as soon as you can name a virtue that brings in as much revenue."

Napoleon despite his status was regarded as very personable in private, with a gentle nature marked by patient kindness and constantly attracted personal devotion. His qualities didn't make him a good ruler, many thought him weak, his foreign policy flawed but some of his domestic and social legislation was remarkably enlightened.

He deliberately drew on symbols of the First Empire and the glories of Bonaparte to underpin his legitimacy.

Eugenie for all her charm, honesty and sincerity was regarded in Palace circles as hot tempered, impetuous and her many "whims" didn't endear her in the same way.

Chapter Three

Hands Across the Sea

Any student of British history will know about the up and down nature of the relationship between France and Britain and this was an era where Waterloo would still be remembered by both sides. A new entente had come about when France and Britain became allies in 1854 to fight the Russians in the Crimean War. This resulted in an invitation to make an official visit to Britain the following April. Both sides were understandably nervous but Napoleon launched a major charm offensive. The Imperial couple spent three days in Windsor and three more at Buckingham Palace. New furniture was bought for the guest bedrooms at Windsor including a splendid red canopied bed, complete with carved cherubs at each corner, a dressing table, wardrobe and chairs!

The highlight was a fabulous ball at the Castle, where Victoria was amazed to be dancing with the nephew of the former great enemy, though the setting, the Waterloo Chamber was renamed for the occasion as the Picture Gallery, but presumably the paintings stayed the same. The significance of the visit was underlined when he was created a Knight of the Order of the Garter and his standard hung in St. George's Chapel, Windsor.

There was a trip to the Opera and a military review which featured some of the horses Napoleon had sent as a present. They also enjoyed a preview of the Crystal Place in its new setting at Sydenham which was captured on an early photograph. More than 100,000 turned up in South London to see the Royals.

Crystal Palace. Smithsonian Institute PD

The Times called the whole tour a "romance of history". Whilst Victoria was generally favourably inclined to the affable Napoleon, she did have some reservations as expressed in a memorandum. "I believe that the Emperor Napoleon would not hesitate to do a thing by main force, even in itself unjust and tyrannical, should he consider that the accomplishment of his destiny demanded it". Prince Albert had greater concerns about his character but both agreed on their warmth towards the Empress. Eugenie had made a major impression as soon as she stepped off the boat at Dover clothed head to foot in Royal Stewart tartan. Banned in Scotland after the battle of Culloden in 1746, tartan had been revived early in the 19th century, boosted by the popularity of Sir Walter Scott's Waverley novels and his romanticised vision of Scotland. It was reinforced by the startling apparition of George IV in full highland regalia on "the King's Jaunt - one and twenty daft days" to Edinburgh in 1822, though the pink stockings he wore under a far too short kilt to keep his legs warm were certainly not regulation wear.

The idea was regarded as textile diplomacy but one Scottish observer thought it a "collective hallucination". It was captured with flattering artistic licence on canvas by Sir David Wilkie.

Victoria had been a regular tartan wearer and Prince Albert adopted the dress in Scotland but Eugenie's outfit sparked a wave of "La Mode L'Ecossaire" and tartanmania even made its way to the United States. Although Eugenie had no royal roots her grandfather, William Kirkpatrick was born in Scotland.

It was an early insight into her future role as a fashion trendsetter but there'd been a major hiccup on the first night. The boat with Eugenie's wardrobe, jewels and hairdresser was delayed by fog and didn't arrive until too late. Eugenie had to borrow a dress from one of her Ladies in waiting, a plain blue silk creation and substituted flowers for jewels. Nonetheless she carried it off as if deliberately planned and the simplicity was much admired.

The success of this tour resulted in a reciprocal trip in August to take in the World Fair. The French had been staging similar domestic events for more than 50 years and their 1849 version was the catalyst for The Great Exhibition in 1851. Numerous British visitors to Paris had returned suggesting Britain could do better on a grander, worldwide scale. Prince Albert had taken it in hand, resulting in probably the greatest achievement of his life as consort.

The French version in 1855 aimed to build on that success and although it made a significant loss it attracted worldwide interest. If the visit to Britain had been grand, significant and well received it seemed understated compared to the extravaganza Napoleon laid on though the British party might have been a little disconcerted by their welcome. They arrived in Boulogne rather later than anticipated so the 21gun salute was fired in the dark which might have been interpreted differently under other circumstances. Flags and banners welcomed the Royal couple into Paris and seemingly every available member of the armed forces was on parade amidst an extraordinary display of pomp and pageantry. It was the first official visit by an English monarch for more than 400 years and the Hundred Years War (think Agincourt and Joan of Arc). Victoria said Paris was the most beautiful and gayest town imaginable and the hard to please Albert was impressed by the improvements since his previous visits. On the other hand, the French press were underwhelmed with Victoria's wardrobe, her clothes weren't a patch on those of the Empress. Maybe Victoria sensed that too as she listed what Eugenie wore in her diary throughout their visit.

The Royal couple stayed in the Imperial apartments at St Cloud and several paintings Victoria had expressed an interest in seeing had been conveniently relocated to her suite from the Louvre. It was an exhaustive and exhausting visit, well received by the huge crowds and Napoleon was an enthusiastic and accommodating guide, the only apparent downside being a heatwave. Eugenie who was in the early stages of pregnancy opted out of some events and was routinely absent from breakfast so was perhaps suffering from morning sickness. Whether Victoria was told of her condition or from her own experience, as a mother of eight by then, just guessed, isn't known but there are oblique references in her diary. You can imagine a womanly tête-à-tête with Victoria passing on handy tips to the suffering Empress, hopefully she skipped too much detail on the indignities and traumas of childbirth, which Eugenie was to experience all too soon.

The Royal couple were accompanied by their two eldest teenage children, Vicky and Bertie (later King Edward VII). Bertie had already developed a rebellious streak and would have found himself, even at 13, in the sad disappointment to his parents' category. He was ecstatic about Paris and the freedoms, the French court was great fun, the opposite of his stuffy home life, the Empress was pretty, kind and attentive and in the pally, smoking, drinking and womanising Emperor he had found a role model for his future indulgences.

Vicky, the Princess Royal was nearly 15 and also found it a life changing experience. She had her own bedroom for the first time in her life and Eugenie had sent her some dresses for the visit. Her measurements had been transferred on to a life sized doll for the purpose. Eugenie had met Vicky on the earlier visit to Windsor and was more attuned to the needs of this young woman than her own mother.

Banquets and balls were the order of the day including a spectacular evening at Versailles, the first Grand Ball there since Louis XIV's time. Napoleon danced with Victoria and Albert with Eugenie. She even persuaded the Queen to let Vicky attend where she danced with the Emperor. She must have suddenly felt very grown up. At the end of the visit to England Eugenie had given Vicky her own diamond and ruby watch and in Paris the Empress gifted her a bejewelled bracelet which included a few strands of her hair. Vicky adored her. Little wonder on the day before they left Bertie and Vicky went to the Empress and asked if they could stay on. "Surely your parents couldn't do without you" she queried "Not do without us" said Bertie "there are six more of us at home and they don't want us". This Prince of Wales would spend a considerable amount of leisure time in Paris in his adult years enjoying the lifestyle and earning the nickname "Dirty Bertie".

At the end of their visit Victoria was genuinely disappointed to leave Paris and especially the Empress, who she described as a fairy like apparition, unlike anyone she had ever seen before. The bond would last their lifetimes

Eugenie's pregnancy was only saved she thought by a trip to the thermal spa waters of the Eaux Bains and the royal heir was duly born in March 1856. It was a traumatic experience. A long agonising two day labour was of great concern to the doctors who at one stage told Napoleon it could be a choice of who lived, the child or his wife. Of course, being a royal birth it had to be witnessed by the necessary courtiers, ministers and a Bonaparte family representative. The indignity must have been great as she writhed in agony, ending up near naked but the child, a boy, was born by forceps around 3am on March 16th after what her doctor described as a most difficult birth. Napoleon

Eugene Louis Jean Joseph Napoleon was known in his early childhood as Lou Lou, later as Louis and officially as the Prince Imperial.

Not everyone was happy, cousin Plon Plon pushed further down the line of succession intensified his dislike of Eugenie.

The birth was signalled by a 100 gun salute and the desired dynasty had been started. It also prompted an amnesty for some of the political prisoners jailed during the early days of the Empire and the Imperial couple announced they would be godparents to every other child born in wedlock in France on the same day. Each would get 3,000 Francs, the boys would be called Louis Eugene and the girls Eugenie-Louise. It was estimated about 3,000 qualified.

Showing off baby. Reine de Moraine . Musée Carnavalet CCØ

The Imperial baptism, three months later in June was a grandiose affair, akin to the coronation Napoleon never had. The procession composed of 12 state carriages with 96 horses and was witnessed by thousands of well-wishers en route to the lavishly decorated Notre Dame where another 6,000 were invited to witness the occasion. A special font made of Sèvres porcelain was filled by a copper baptismal ewer dating back to the 12th Century Crusades. The young heir's god parents were Pope Pius IX, in absentia and Queen Josephine of Sweden and the celebrations, balls and fireworks lasted for three days.

Meanwhile, Eugenie was still suffering, the result was a warning from the doctors that any further pregnancies would be dangerous to her health and potentially fatal and for months this was underlined by her inability to walk unaided whilst her body healed. She was to suffer with back pain for years as a consequence of the birth trauma. It left Napoleon with an obvious excuse to act as he wished. He later said "Where women are concerned I do not believe in attack, I defend myself and sometimes I yield". Whilst Eugenie could hardly make a public scene about his behaviour her outward acceptance wasn't mirrored behind closed doors and Napoleon, who shied away from arguments must have had a rough time!

Throughout their marriage Napoleon would call her Genie, and address her using the informal version of "you", which according to French grammar rules is "tu", Eugenie would call him Louis rather than Napoleon and use the formal version "vous", a reflection of his status.

After the success of the Royal visits in 1855 the Imperial couple visited Osborne in July 1857 but political business was on the agenda. No matter how friendly relations had become, six months later on Jan 14th 1858 it suffered a blip when an anarchist, Felice Orsini tried to assassinate the Imperial couple as they rode to the opera. Orsini was a prominent campaigner for Italian Independence and regarded French foreign policy as the barrier to that outcome. He and two fellow revolutionaries threw bombs at the Imperial carriage and although Napoleon and Eugenie were unhurt and defiantly continued to the performance, eight were killed and more than 140 injured. Eugenie's dress was spattered with blood from a small cut.

Orsini was captured and guillotined but he'd been living freely in England and the bombs had been made in Birmingham with support from some English radicals. The French demanded Britain should act to restrict the right to asylum but a conspiracy bill was defeated in Parliament and the Government resigned. Those conspirators still in Britain escaped jail.

There were other niggling disagreements between the two states and in an attempt to restore better relations Napoleon invited Victoria and Albert to witness the opening of the new naval base at Cherbourg in August 1858. It was an impressive site, the biggest in the world and here was the French navy out in force just 90 miles from the English coast, Nelson would have been spinning in his sarcophagus in St Paul's. Victoria may have been greeted with flags and fireworks but she was extremely worried by what she saw and curtailed the trip. She also let her feelings known to her government, not quite the reaction either country had anticipated.

Fortunately, Napoleon's military attentions were elsewhere, partly looking south to Italy spurred on perhaps by his mistress, an infamous fame fatale.

In late 1855 the Count and Countess di Castiglione arrived in Paris. It was a loveless, arranged marriage and the Countess was instructed by her cousin, the influential Italian minister Count Cavour, to influence Napoleon in their favour "succeed by whatever means you wish - but succeed". Her weapon was her looks, she was reputedly the greatest beauty of the age and didn't she know it. Her long, wavy blonde hair and pale skin was coupled with mesmerising eyes that changed colour from green to blue-violet. Napoleon needed no encouragement. She was first presented at a court ball on January 9th 1856, she was 18 and Eugenie was heavily pregnant. La Castiglione, as she was known, was described as having "wonderful hair, the waist of a nymph, and a complexion the colour of pink marble! In a word, Venus descended from Olympus". She was vanity personified and would appear late at balls, stand centre stage as the men fawned over her whilst ignoring the women who regarded her with a mixture of jealousy and contempt. She had everything except that great essential, charm. Her most famous outfit was worn at a fancy dress ball the following year when she came as the Queen of Hearts on the arm of the Emperor. The gold muslin dress dotted with gold hearts was almost entirely see-through, and she wasn't wearing a corset, leaving little to the imagination.

The attendees gasped and the Empress made her feelings known to her face, "The heart is a little low, madam," a polite way of suggesting there was far too much on show.

Virgine Castiglione later gave birth to a boy, reputedly fathered by the Emperor, and he was said to bear a striking resemblance to the Prince Imperial. Known as Arthur Hugenschmidt he was taken under the wing of the Imperial dentist Dr Thomas Evans and followed him into the profession. Eugenie would

La Castiglione. Queen of Hearts.
Met Museum PD

meet him several times in later years. Who knows how many other little Napoleons were running round Paris.

La Castiglione's continual extravagance led her cuckolded husband to bankruptcy and divorce. She left Paris but returned a few years later acting more like an old fashioned courtesan, (a high class paid escort). Eventually as her beauty faded, she became a recluse and increasingly eccentric only ever appearing at night, heavily veiled. She had the mirrors removed from her house and the walls painted black but her place in posterity was guaranteed as during her heyday she'd had hundreds of studio photos taken, many in her famous costumes, all carefully directed by herself and destined to preserve her fame.

It's unlikely La Castiglione had any influence on the Emperor, he was attracted by her body not her brains but in 1859 he took action against Austria who controlled the northern part of Italy. The Emperor who'd trained with the Swiss army led the French campaign with many battle hardened troops from the Crimea, leaving Eugenie as Regent. The decisive battle occurred south of Lake Garda at Solferino in June 1859. The French not wishing to risk an escalation and war with Prussia then signed an armistice and left. One unexpected consequence was the founding some years later of the Red Cross. A Swiss businessman and social activist Henry Dunant had visited the battlefield after the fighting and seen the wounded soldiers left there to die. He published his account in "A Memory of Solferino" which led to the creation of the International Red Cross in 1863, the Geneva Convention followed a year later based on Dunant's idea for an independent organisation to care for wounded soldiers.

Eugenie enjoyed her three month Regency and sitting in on the councils gave her an insight and appetite for foreign affairs.

Not content with their European adventures France had teamed up again with Britain in the 2nd Opium War against China in 1860. It culminated in the controversial looting of the Summer Palace in Peking (Beijing) where thousands of high value items were stolen. Plunder was nothing new as the soldiers would sell their treasures to earn money. The author, Victor Hugo described it as a barbaric act and the two countries as bandits. Many prized artefacts taken by the French ended up at the Palace of Fontainebleau in the Chinese Museum. One of the presents given to Queen Victoria was a small dog from a previously unknown breed which became classified as Pekingese. Victoria appropriately named the dog, Looty.

Chapter Four

A New Home

Whilst most of their life was spent in and around Paris, Napoleon decided to build a summer home in Biarritz in South West France where Eugenie had enjoyed holidays before their marriage. This was just a small fishing village on the Atlantic coast when building began but the Villa Eugenie gave the Empress more freedom and an opportunity to enjoy her love of the countryside.

Villa Eugenie – Photos courtesy of Les Pyrénées Basques

Shaped in the form of an E, it was constructed on the dunes and was a fairly simple residence by royal standards. One English visitor in 1858 was totally underwhelmed, noting it commanded "an extensive view of the cruel grey expanse of the Bay of Biscay; the really beautiful landscape towards the Spanish frontier being carefully excluded".

For six weeks in late summer most years Eugenie could escape the pressures of Paris and indulge in another of her pleasures, the luxury of an early morning swim in the sea. Dressed in a voluminous costume she would go far enough away from land to avoid prying eyes and telescopes, always escorted by some reliable fisherman and preferably when a storm was brewing.

In the summer of 1858 the young Prince Imperial was taken ill and Eugenie sent his governess from Biarritz to Lourdes 100 miles away to bring back some water from the Lady's grotto. This was the scene of several visions of the Virgin Mary and the spring water was famed for its healing properties. The Mayor, had ordered the area to be fenced off but the governess ignored the barriers and was arrested. When she explained her mission, she was released and when the Prince recovered Napoleon ordered the barricades to be removed. The locals were delighted and Lourdes attracts thousands of pilgrims each year with many recorded miracle healings.

The guest list at the Villa Eugenie was strictly limited and any important political discussions could be held in the more relaxed atmosphere. In 1859, Eugenie took around 50 guests on a mountain walk/climb up La Rhune in the Pyrenees. It was to turn into a testing outward bound expedition and most were totally unprepared for the challenge ahead.

Carriages took them part way before they transferred to mules and in line with the Basque custom the guests were paired up size wise into what could best be described as pannier style chairs, one on each side of the animal. Given the women were encased in crinolines it certainly sounds uncomfortable and as the mules had a tendency to wander off the straight and narrow paths, very disconcerting and most of the party decided to walk the last stretch to their lunchtime picnic. Eugenie had come dressed as simply as protocol allowed in a red jacket and black wool skirt but with a Spanish style black hat with two pom poms. Prompted by the arrival of some local musicians she couldn't resist the temptation to demonstrate the Fandango complete with castanets. It was, according to one guest a graceful, charming and enthusiastic performance of her Spanish National dance, full of Andalusian spirit. The entertainment over they then had to finish the climb, another two hours to the summit at 3,000 feet, (905 metres) and a few steps from the Spanish border. After admiring the fabulous view Eugenie teasingly walked past the border post and crossed into her homeland.

Rather late in the day they began the return journey, some decided to walk, others out of desperation resorted once more to the mules. As darkness fell, many began to flounder, the pathway was barely visible and when one collapsed an improvised stretcher had to be made. This caused mutiny in the ranks as others then demanded the same and tree branches had to be cut down to make them. It's hard to imagine what tools they had with them to facilitate this operation. Eventually at 10pm they reached the waiting carriages, few had escaped unscarred, the court shoes of the great ladies had long since disintegrated and only

Eugenie and a soon to be newcomer to court, an Austrian Princess, Pauline Metternich, used to mountain terrain were still in a fit state to step into a carriage unaided. The Empress agreed that she hadn't been selective enough in inviting the guests for such a day out and proposed the next picnic would be at sea.

The chosen craft was a naval despatch boat, the Seagull and 52 guests, many from the infamous mountain adventure had signed up. The women were dressed in their fashionable frocks, the men in top hats and formal coats and all anticipated a leisurely excursion on a beautiful day. Seated on deck in their wicker chairs they could contemplate the prospect of a sumptuous afternoon tea on their picturesque cruise to Fuenterrabia. What could possibly go wrong? Well pretty much everything.

As they set sail just after 2pm all seemed set fair, though the small boats bobbing up and down in the harbour might have been a warning sign to those in the know. Their voyage was to take them across the Bay of Biscay, notorious for its fickle weather conditions which had lured many unsuspecting landlubbers into its clutches. Gradually conditions worsened as the Seagull battled against the increasingly angry waves and the once happy faces turned a mix of ashen white and green. Only Eugenie who rarely seemed to suffer from mal de mer (seasickness) was unperturbed, the rest succumbed, the smell of food being the last straw. Some lay down as best they could to alleviate the motion sickness, which left the Empress to tend to their needs. This was a warship not a cruise liner and totally unsuited for such a crisis. The steamer ploughed on and when the Empress announced she could see their destination and they would drive back to Biarritz the near dead seemed to revive. They gingerly transferred into the small boats that were to take them to the sanctuary of dry land but after only a few minutes the crews decided it was too dangerous and turned round. The pitching and rolling Seagull headed back to Biarritz to be greeted by a rocket display as they neared safety. The desperate passengers regarded them as them welcoming fireworks, how thoughtful, sadly it was the complete opposite. The pilot, well bribed by Napoleon to brave the conditions, climbed on board with a message from the Emperor forbidding them to land as it was too dangerous. They must go back out to sea and the Captain must not enter any port unless he could do so without running the slightest risk.

Six hours passed before the Empress asked the Captain if he could try a landing further down the coast. At 2am they were signalled landward by the harbourmaster at the entrance to the River Adour but now the officers and crew were themselves anxious as there was little margin of error in steering the course. They openly discussed how they could save the Empress if they were shipwrecked. Most guests said their prayers, many wailed in desperation as the waves crashed over the vessel but by some miracle the helmsman steered the Seagull through the narrow channel to safety. The Emperor, who had summoned the carriages and ridden down the coast was on the quayside watching in alarm as the Empress came ashore. Beside himself with anger and relief he forbid her from any more such escapades, a sentiment echoed secretly by everyone else. The bedraggled party with clothes torn to rags fell into the waiting carriages to be driven slowly back to Villa Eugenie.

Not every summer was so dangerous, Eugenie was a devotee of the local spas and their sulphurous thermal waters. Her patronage led to a town being created in her honour, Eugenie-Les-Bains. It is one of many such resorts in the area.

Chapter Five

A New Friend and a New Fashion

Princess Pauline Metternich.
Musée Carnavalet CCØ

At the end of 1859, a social whirlwind, Princess Pauline Metternich, the wife of the new Austrian Ambassador blew into Paris. Given the French had been at war with Austria only a few months before this must have been a tricky situation.

She was outgoing, cultured, not by her own admission pretty but renowned for her fashionable good taste. Her behaviour on the other hand bordered on the outrageous, verging repeatedly on social impropriety and some regarded her as a bad influence on Eugenie. Years later when Metternich was back in Vienna it was alleged she fought a topless duel with an Austrian Countess over a floral decoration. Although she vehemently denied it, those who had known her in Paris were unconvinced. Nevertheless, she took her place as a leading member of French society and was instrumental in changing the world of fashion.

At the start of the Empire the two pre-eminent couturiers and Fournisseurs breveté (Royal warrant holders), were Madame Vignon and Madame Palmyre. They'd supplied 54 dresses for Eugenie's wedding trousseau which given the time scale between the engagement and wedding must have been a frenetic process. Whilst they continued to produce clothes for Eugenie it was the man who'd supplied much of the fabric who was to steal the limelight.

The arrival at court of Princess Pauline inspired an enterprising young British dressmaker Charles Frederick Worth to gain an audience with her. He wasn't unknown, he'd won a 1st class medal for one of his designs at the 1855 World Fair and then opened his own business but he knew such a client would enhance his status. He sent his wife Marie with his portfolio to gain an audience, Metternich was immediately impressed with his designs and wore one his gowns to the opening ball of the season at the Tuileries. It was a turning point.

Eugenie, who had taken a liking to Metternich and not just for her mountain climbing, was keen to know who had made the dress. She might have been surprised to find it was an Englishman but Worth was summoned to the Palace the following morning, "he was made and I was lost" joked Metternich "for from that moment they'll be no more dresses at 300 francs". It was a watershed for Worth who is now regarded as the father of Haute Couture and for Eugenie, who was to be catapulted to the forefront of world fashion.

Worth was born in Lincolnshire and after his drunken solicitor father had squandered the family money he'd been apprenticed in London as a sales assistant at a department store called Swan and Edgar.

Largely self-taught he would study the clothes of the rich and famous from previous eras by examining the portraits in the recently opened National Gallery. It was the age of the dandy, richly and flamboyantly dressed men about town, women's fashions in England had no such equivalent and were generally dull and dreary, one dress, a shawl and a bonnet. Any innovations were born in Paris and so he followed that trail, despite knowing no one and unable to speak the language.

It was a frustrating experience at first as dressmaking was almost exclusively a women's world but eventually Worth was allowed to develop his own methods and designs. After starting his own atelier (workshop/showroom) his wife would model his creations, a novel idea, later he was the first to add a maker's label to his work. His clients, except the Empress were expected to come to him and he generally relied on a single fitting but uniquely modelled his new creations on real women chosen to represent his regular clients. Orders flooded in from around the world.

He was certainly different, he arrived at the Palace but not in the required court dress, instead everyday clothes and a beret. Eugenie wasn't really a fashionista at heart and when not on show dressed quite simply but knew that her position required her to set a stylish example. She ordered one dress and then entire wardrobes and the journals all round the world picked up on what she wore and the social elites followed suit. Most designers in the period slavishly followed the wishes of their clients, Worth wanted to lead and even Eugenie had to give way. On one occasion he produced a dress of heavy woven brocade from Lyon, the Empress objected saying it would make her look like a curtain. The Emperor was called in to adjudicate and supported Worth as it ensured more work for the troublesome Lyon weavers. Many of the future designs would help to stimulate French industry. Worth was also keen to bring in changes of style, no longer the slight variations on a theme, every year a new collection would be launched and woe betide the fashion conscious appearing in last year's outfits. His main showrooms would include a room with mirrored walls, lit by gaslight which would show the intricate and delicate workmanship under ball like conditions. Assisted by well dressed handsome young male shop assistants it was all designed to attract potential clients.

This was the era of the crinoline but contrary to popular belief they weren't invented by Worth, in fact he wasn't too keen.

House of Worth. Met Museum PD

By the mid 1850's there were large factories in Paris and London producing the hoop like frames, initially of whalebone but later of steel.

The skirts themselves grew in dimension with some reaching nearly two metres in circumference, an early form of social distancing. At their height of popularity, a factory could produce several thousand a day. They might have been fashionable but they were increasingly impractical. Whilst the steel frame meant fewer petticoats, the spring in the frame could, after a sudden movement by the wearer reveal much more than was intended. In general, they were severely inhibiting, try getting through a crowd or a door.

On one occasion a Papal representative arrived at a ball to find his way blocked by two ladies with enormous crinolines. "Pardon Monsignor, but there is so much material in our skirts" said one, "that there is nothing left for the top" quipped his eminence.

When the Royals met up in Cherbourg, a French minister gave orders to widen the gangplanks and stairs on the Imperial yacht to accommodate the dresses. Whilst the graceful Eugenie could carry off the fashion and no one dare to criticise her, one observer had some cruel words for Victoria and her entourage, "the ladies from Osborne appeared to walk in portly tubs".

Happiness and Misfortune. Musée Carnavalet   CCØ

Less publicised were the dangers of wearing a crinoline with hundreds of deaths each year caused by accidents including most alarmingly by being burnt alive if the wearer erred too near a lit candle, open fire, or was hit by a stray spark. Another dangerous trend was the "tightlacing" of corsets which squeezed the waist narrower but which could cause internal damage. The Empress, described surprisingly as "stout" by her corsetier didn't indulge in this as her 27inch waist was proportionate to her bust but unusually she wore a lightweight night corset to maintain her figure. She had excellent posture, definitely no slouching when sitting down.

Her dresses were stored in an attic room inside huge wardrobes so they could be put on a wicker dummy and lowered down by a form of lift into her dressing room. New dresses would be assembled on these life sized dolls so she could judge their suitability and ladies were employed to try on an outfit prior to an event to make sure everything was in order.

New colours emerged such as Mauve and in 1864 Eugenie appeared at the opera in a spectacular emerald green dress, impressive enough to make the headlines as it had the added bonus the colour wasn't diluted by the light from the gas lamps. Suddenly everyone wanted materials in this shade, not just dresses but wallpaper too. The only problem was the pigment in this "Paris Green" contained a significant amount of arsenic and the toxicity resulted in severe illness and even death in some of those who worked closely with it.

Worth continued to work with the crinoline until the late 1860's before the bustle took over but he'd already made several variations and was always pushing the boundaries. There was a slightly shorter dress for walking and a much shorter knee length version for skating with wide velvet knickerbockers underneath which buttoned below the knee. Complete with gaiters which covered the calf, the fur trimmed outfit would avoid any embarrassment should the skater fall over.

In 1867 for a state visit to Salzburg, Worth created a dress that only went down as far as her ankles. It was very practical as the official welcome was at the station so he didn't want it to drag along the ground but it sent shockwaves through the fashion world. Within days the news had spread across the Atlantic and into the pages of 'Godey's Lady book', the American fashion Bible. Amongst those who were keen followers of her style was Mary Todd, wife of the President, Abraham Lincoln but her rather dumpy figure didn't suit the fashions nearly so well.

The Salzburg visit was the first time Eugenie had met the Austrian Empress, "Sisi". She too was regarded as a great beauty and was 10 years younger so many thought it would lead to some intense rivalry, but instead they hit it off. One evening Sisi went round for a private talk with Eugenie. Rather improbably they decided to compare their vital statistics using some royal ribbons as tape measures. Both parties must have been satisfied with the outcome as the pair became firm friends.

Naturally every royal outfit needed the appropriate accessories and Eugenie could choose from an extensive collection of exquisite jewellery. The Fontenay Tiara (overleaf) made in 1858 was set with Emeralds, not the Sapphires depicted in the painting. Often pieces would be reworked and reset during the Empire.

Minature by Pommayrac
art.thewalters.org CCØ

When it came to hats, Eugenie's milliners also ensured she was a trend setter. Whilst ostrich feathers had been incorporated into hats for decades, in the late 1860's she wore one which featured stuffed humming birds. The growth in the hunting and selling of exotic birds had been fuelled by the demands of the hat trade. The anti-plumage campaigners termed it "murderous millinery" as hundreds of thousands of birds, especially egrets, birds of paradise and humming birds were killed and sold by the tray load each year well up to the First World War. The campaigning led to the eventual foundation of the (Royal) Society for the protection of birds.

In the 1930's the "Eugenie" hat named after the Empress was in vogue. Worn by film stars such as Greta Garbo it was originally designed for riding or travel. Made usually of velvet or felt, the hat was often decorated with a feather and tilted forwards or over one side of the face - très chic.

In 1853 a perfume company produced an Eau de Cologne in a gold bottle patterned with embossed bees. The symbol was another of Bonaparte's ideas as bees represented the virtues of industry and hard work and was also the oldest emblem of a French sovereign dating back to the 5th century.

The social highlights of the season were the Imperial balls and they required the services of another highly sought after genius, a stocky, middle aged fellow called Leroy, the hairdresser. Society ladies would wait anxiously, their hair in "papers" (curlers), sometimes for hours, he would then breeze in and like some magician in a matter of minutes create the required effect. All well and good but if you were one of his morning clients you then had to sit around for the rest of the day trying not to disturb his handiwork before heading off to a ball. Eugenie would often add gold powder to her hair to give it a burnished look but such was Leroy's fame he once rejected her request for an appointment, lured by an extravagant offer to perform in Berlin.

Of course, you needed that all important invite to the ball but how did you get one if you hadn't been introduced at court. In the case of Lillie Moulton, an American socialite living in the millionaire quarter of Paris it was her prowess as an ice skater.

In January 1863 one of the small lakes in the Bois de Boulogne froze over and Parisians rushed out to have a look. Having been brought up in the cold winters of Massachusetts, Lillie was an experienced skater and whilst others assessed the possibilities she sailed onto the ice, as she described in an excited letter to her mother. "I skimmed over the flawless ice on the outer edge, like a bird with close-fitting wings; indeed, I felt like one. The ice was so clear that one could see the grass and stones at the bottom. This was an exhilarating moment!" A second circuit with her young child in her arms was regarded with amazement and caught the attention of the Emperor who was struggling and slithering uncertainly on the ice. He asked her to partner him across the pond which was a nerve wracking experience for her but despite losing his top hat he didn't fall over. She was then introduced to the Empress and guided her around the makeshift rink. What followed was a request to skate with her the next day and teach the Prince Imperial plus an invitation to the season's first ball.

There were four or five winter balls at the Tuileries from January to Lent each with around 4-5000 guests. Since white was the regulation colour Moulton wore her wedding dress and would have been made aware of the strict rules, no dress could be worn more than once and if you weren't sufficiently well attired you would be warned or even turned away and not invited again. Many of those who attended were unfamiliar with the necessary etiquette so guidebooks were available to help them meet the required standards.

The men wore white knee breeches, white stockings and a dress coat unless they were in uniform. Napoleon had reinstated old fashioned court dress but this retro look had a comic opera feel to the end result. The court officials were also required to wear embroidered coats with braided sleeves and double pointed hats, sometimes with swords which added to the discomfort. It also caused rivalry between departments and to be honest not many middle aged men look good in knee breeches and silk stockings.

The ordinary guests would arrive by carriage which queued up outside the Tuileries, sometimes taking more than an hour to reach the front. The privileged would have a different entrance and staircase, no crumpled crinolines squashed in the rush for them. There was food but never enough.

Once inside, the normal guests would climb the staircase lined by the Imperial bodyguards, standing like statues on each step before being guided specifically to their designated place. The dancing would be held in two rooms so needed a double orchestra. The main space was the immense Salle des Maréchaux with the portraits of 12 Bonaparte Generals on the walls and the enormous caryatids (large Greek style statues) by the entrance. The entire ballroom was lit with wax candles which sounds like a scene from Cinderella and there was certainly a fairytale element to it. At one end was the platform with the Imperial thrones and behind them red velvet hangings displaying the gold Napoleonic eagle. The other members of the family were seated on a row of red velvet and gilt chairs.

Imperial Ball at the Tuileries. Wood engraving Charles Mourand after
Gustave Janet. Wellcome Collection PD

At 10pm the Imperial party arrived having enjoyed a private supper,
the audience bowed and Eugenie responded with a series of her
trademark deep, sweeping curtsies. The Empress would only dance
the opening quadrille at 1030, the couple would then mingle from
1100 and normally leave at midnight but guests could stay for two or
three hours more.

Whilst Moulton was in awe of the whole event she received an
unexpected summons from the Empress and was almost overcome
with nerves as she felt the eyes of the entire ballroom on her, wondering
why this newcomer had received special attention. "As this was the
first time I had seen her in evening dress, I was completely dazed by
her loveliness and beauty. I can't imagine a more beautiful apparition
than she was. Her delicate colouring, the pose of her head, her hair,
her expressive mouth, her beautiful shoulders, and wonderful
grace make a perfect ensemble...when I glazed at her I could hardly
believe that we had been such chums a few days before, when skating,

and that I had held her hands clasped in mine, and had kept her from falling".

Such balls could be exhausting and for the Imperial couple probably pretty boring but the Empress always seemed pristine and had an enviable memory for names and faces. The many fabulous jewels she wore were heavy so she was quick to remove them once she returned to her apartments, sometimes almost throwing them at a Lady in waiting.

The New Year celebrations were a two day marathon with women required to add a long train to their dresses and parade and curtsy in front of the Imperial couple. After Easter there were smaller events known as the Empress's Mondays held in the private apartments but Eugenie's favourite were the costume balls normally held before Christmas with one at the Tuileries but most elsewhere in the city. She would wear some extravagant and often exotic costumes, occasionally in the National dress of other countries. These were called "Les Travestis" and were far removed from her Imperial wardrobe. She, like La Castiglione had studio photographs taken, (a limited edition) perhaps designed to remind her of some fun filled evenings.

At the end of each season Eugenie's wardrobe would be sold off, the dresses would be stripped of their jewels and bought by ladies in waiting or staff primed by fashion conscious outsiders. Her Spanish maid Pepa had first choice and would make a handsome bonus from their sale. As the Empress had small feet, size 3, her shoes were given away to a local orphanage for the young girls to wear at their confirmations.

If the expenditure on fashion seemed excessive, remarkably Eugenie kept an account of her spending and would later say she stuck to a strict budget. Whilst she had to maintain an Imperial standard of dress in public, her day wear was much simpler and she would often go out in her carriage with a plain dress under a more expensive shawl or jacket to give the regal effect.

Her allowance was fr120,000 of which only fr20,000 was spent on clothes. Much of the rest went in charitable donations.

Eugenie. Musée Carnavalet CCØ

Chapter Six

On Tour

In 1860 the Imperial couple went on a tour through southern France and then on to Corsica (birthplace of the great Bonaparte) ending in the French colony of Algeria. The French had invaded Algiers in 1830 after a greatly exaggerated political snub and gradually expanded their colonial holdings, aided by the presence of the Foreign Legion who made the country their home from 1831. During the tour Eugenie's sister Paca, who'd been ill for a while, died. The news was deliberately withheld until near the end of the visit which meant it was too late for the Empress to return to Paris for the funeral on September 20th. She was inconsolable.

Her misery was compounded by court life and supposedly another of her husband's dalliances, and on November 14th she suddenly left Paris for England. The official, belated statement explained that her doctors had advised her to take a rest and holiday to recover from her sister's death and that Napoleon waved her off at the Gare de Nord. Less charitable sources suggest Eugenie just upped and left with four members of her close entourage and a handful of servants leaving her 4 year old son behind. She travelled incognito under the alias of the Comtesse des Pierrefonds, named after a Castle north east of Paris which the couple were having restored. That title was to be used on numerous occasions in the future.

Eugenie took the boat train, arrived at London Bridge station and took a taxi to a hotel, but which one, some reports mention that as she hadn't booked in advance the party tried a couple of options before arriving at Claridges in Mayfair.

The hotel was none the wiser as to her true identity and the British government were equally unaware of her trip, nor of her plans to visit Scotland. The following morning she popped out on foot to do some shopping around nearby Bond St.

Her journey north wasn't quite up to regal standards, despite being in First Class it was a slow steam train in an unheated carriage which required the party to wrap up well. Eugenie broke her journey in York, visited the famous Minster and arrived in Edinburgh on Saturday November 17th but by now her cover was blown. If Scotland seems a strange choice to visit in mid November she could point to her grandfather's Scottish roots, but more importantly she also sought medical advice from Dr James Young Simpson. He was an eminent physician and Eugenie feared her bad back could be symptomatic of the illness which had killed her sister so was keen to get his opinion.

Eugenie then went into full tourist mode, she began by visiting Holyrood Palace though the wintry weather denied her the opportunity to climb to the top of Arthur's seat. It was followed by a whistle stop tour of the country and at nearly every station the locals seemed to know in advance who she was and came out to cheer her on. Her destinations included Sir Walter Scott's home at Abbotsford, Loch Lomond, Perth, Stirling and Blair Castle though that wasn't without incident. The Castle was closed up and the Duke of Atholl, who was living at his winter residence in Dunkeld had to show her round in the dark using candles before she returned to her hotel by moonlight.

The following evening the Duke sent his two best pipers Aeneas and William Rose to the Birnam Hotel. They positioned themselves below her sitting room window and played a selection of tunes whilst she dined, before being invited in and introduced to the Empress.

Her presence in Scotland led to an invitation to a forthcoming ball at Hamilton Palace, the imposing seat of the Hamilton family, the premiere Dukedom of Scotland. The Duchess was Princess Marie of Baden, a cousin of Napoleon and they were regular visitors to Paris.

They'd seen the Empress there a few days before her trip but had no idea of her impending visit.

Hamilton Palace was one of the grandest houses in Britain with more rooms than Buckingham Palace and news of her attendance brought a huge crowd to the park to see her arrive. The Hamiltons thought it highly unlikely that Eugenie had bolted as it would have endangered her position as Empress but who knows. (Sadly, the Palace is no more, it was demolished in 1921, in part due to mining excavations under the house).

Her return to London was via Manchester where she was invited by the local council to see the glories of the city's industrial fame. The details, like many of her life and travels, were in a syndicated report picked up worldwide including in the "Bathurst Freepress and Mining Journal" of New South Wales, Australia a few months later. "The weather was as bad as could be hoped for, even in Manchester. A thick, hazy atmosphere, something improving to undoubted fog; above, mist always. Driving rain frequently; below, sloppy mud covering roads and footways. Nothing distinct to the eyes, nothing comfortable to the feelings. Yet even on such a day the Empress of the French, as all who were near her majesty will unhesitatingly assert enjoyed herself in Manchester most unmistakably. Her Majesty said since she left Paris ill and unnerved, from circumstances under which all could sympathise with her. If so, the change of scene and the atmosphere of Great Britain have exerted restorative powers of a very wonderful kind. For throughout her long day's work, it was work that would have overcome many a supposed healthy and hearty lady, the Empress showed unceasing affability to every one of every class whom she came near; unwearying curiosity as to all she saw, and the frankest power of being pleased that was perhaps ever witnessed."

She continued south, stopping in Royal Leamington Spa where her husband had spent the winter of 1838/9 whilst in exile. She then returned to Claridges and was soon invited to Windsor. The weather was again dreadful and Victoria was troubled by Eugenie's appearance "She looked thin & pale & unusually melancholy but was as kind, sensible & natural, as she has always been…. She talked a good deal of her journey, with which she was much pleased, but when she spoke of her return from Algeria, her eyes filled with tears & she said that it was only since she had come here that she had been able to sleep & eat again…she gave me such a melancholy impression, as if some deep grief & anxiety weighed upon her. Poor thing, one must feel much for her". **(1)**

Eugenie did manage to enjoy some of the sights of London including a tour of the new reading room at the British Museum, the Tower of London and a trip to Madame Tussauds, in each case arriving unannounced. Her visit was rounded off by a reciprocal visit from the Queen who arrived at the hotel after visiting a Cattle show in Baker Street. Met at the hotel door they presumably enjoyed a cup of tea and Victoria thought her much improved "She looked very pretty & was in better spirits, telling us all she had seen, but again never mentioning the Empr or Politics. She remains a little longer, & it is evident she likes being here". **(2)**

Eugenie returned to Paris three days later seemingly in much better heart and there was some form of reconciliation but the house she had built for Paca's visits to Paris was too awful a reminder of her death and was demolished.

18 months later the Loch Lomond Steamboat company were surprised to receive two oval Sèvres porcelain vases in recognition of their "attention and courtesy". They'd provided her with a private boat to tour the Loch and the reward was the mauve, gold handled 2 ½ foot high vases.

If her tour reinforced continental views of British weather, the pipers had made a more positive impression. The following year the Duke of Atholl and some friends were invited to Compiègne and received some specific instructions, as at the bottom of the invitation were the words,

'And bring Rose, the piper, with you.' Their appearance certainly left a major impression as Bagpipe News reported. "Rose was instructed to go to the Empress's boudoir with his pipes. All the gentlemen were in Highland costume, and the Empress and most of the French ladies present wore the Atholl tartan in honour of the Duke. When we went in the Empress shook hands with him, took the pipes, stating that she was to show to the ladies, and this she did. At the request of the Empress, he played a reel, which was danced by eight couples, Her Imperial Highness asking the Duke to be her partner". Prosper Mérimée was evidently shocked at the Scottish dancing. "Eight naked knees in the drawing room, the devilish music and the turning, jumping and very alarming tossing of the kilts". The Scots obviously enjoyed themselves, whilst those above stairs went hunting the servants were given free passes to the Paris theatres. Dressed in their Highland costume they must have created quite a stir but were frequently greeted with cheers and shouts of "les braves Ecossaises." The following year the Duke's party were invited back where Eugenie demonstrated her skill with a gun, bagging eight pheasants. One of them she gave to Rose, which was stuffed and subsequently displayed at his home in Dunkeld for all to see, becoming a prized family heirloom.

Each year Compiègne would host a series of invitees where 80 to 100 guests from many different walks of life would spend eight days at the Chateau. In November 1857 the British Foreign Secretary, Lord Clarendon, asked Lord Cowley to give him some idea of what life was like at these house parties. "It is difficult to describe", the Ambassador replied, with a distinct lack of enthusiasm: "Breakfast is at 11, then there is either hunting or shooting, or some expedition. Dinner about 8 o'clock, which never lasts more than an hour. In the evening there is dancing to a hand organ (a dreadful trial to one's auricular nerves) or charades or cards. The hand organ is employed because the Emperor fancies that regular musicians would tell tales – so a wretched chamberlain has to grind all evening".

Cowley may not have liked the entertainment but he loved the hunting. In 1865 he shot nearly 300 game, mainly rabbits and hares plus a few deer. Watching this carnage was the famous microbiologist Louis Pasteur who thought it barbaric. He was there to present his report on the disease that was devastating vineyards throughout Europe. He was delighted at the knowledge and genuine interest in all his work by the Imperial couple who requested a private demonstration of what became known as pasteurisation, heating a liquid to kill the dangerous microbes. After an hour they moved next door to the tea room to perform a party trick for some of the other guests. The Empress enthusiastically carried some of the equipment acting like a humble lab assistant. He was to show his audience the difference between a frog's blood and human blood and immediately Eugenie pricked her finger to provide the required sample. It was the first time most of the guests would have seen a microscope and they were keen to see the blood of the Empress. He was clearly won over by her.

Around the same time as Pasteur's visit Lillie Moulton was invited to join the party goers and gave it an enthusiastic review though was staggered to see most of the town's 12,000 inhabitants waiting at the station to gawp at them. The guests were then taken to the chateau in a series of 10 charabancs (horse drawn coaches). The excessive amount of luggage needed its own transport, her personal wardrobe included eight day costumes, a riding habit for hunting, seven ball dresses and five tea gowns. These had all come from Worth so it was an expensive holiday. Despite being used to the Tuileries, and although the party was supposed to be comparatively informal, Mrs Moulton found herself a little daunted by the grandeur of Compiègne. The Cent Gardes (Imperial bodyguards) were very much in evidence, 50 footmen with powdered hair in red and white liveries served dinner and a military band in the courtyard played throughout the meal. Amateur theatre was particularly appreciated with guests participating in charades, pantomimes, and Lillie, an accomplished amateur singer was often called on to perform, including some American songs requested by Napoleon including Nelly Bly and Swanee River.

The Compiègne parties cost 10,000 francs a day to run with an astonishing 900 people to feed, however as the guests prepared to leave they were in for a shock as they were presented with a huge bill of 600 francs for tips. Eventually a guest complained to the papers and the Emperor, who was unaware of the practice, banned all tipping. The next year Lillie eagerly accepted another invitation to Compiègne though had to implore her millionaire father-in-law to pay the clothes bill.

Lillie was out of the country in August 1864 so missed the extravagant fete at Versailles for the King Consort of Spain, husband of Queen Isabella II which marked the opening of a new rail link between the countries. It was described by one paper as the most lavish since the days of Louis XIV, another thought it a "fairy drama".

Eugenie was determined to impress her fellow Spaniard and money was no object. Princess Metternich joined her on a planning visit and listened in disbelief as the details were discussed for the lighting of the park. "Rows of fairy lights were to be laid everywhere, all the fountains were to be illuminated with arc lamps, whilst electric searchlights were to be installed on the roof of the Palace to project their rays on the entire flower garden below. All the trees were to be illuminated with Red and Orange bulbs which would convey the impression they were bearing luminous fruit, and a million and half were to be employed". Quite how this was done isn't clear, electricity is mentioned but not as we know it, Bengal fires, a sort of flare candle and resin fires are listed. Whatever the mechanics, the result was breath taking.

Nocturne at Versailles August 21ˢᵗ 1864

Metternich was unimpressed with the King of Spain who was, "without exception, the most insignificant creature imaginable; physically utterly unworthy of the magnificent fete arranged in his honour"! After a private supper they watched a play in the Palace theatre before the fireworks began at 11pm. The crowds flocked into the park to marvel at the spectacle of 100,000 rockets, beginning with the coat of arms of France and Spain, engineered by Ruggiero, the pyrotechnic king. The Telegraph reported "for half an hour, the heaven was a galaxy of coloured stars; gold and silver fell around us. Rainbows seemed to rise above us and then burst into particles of colour. The Spanish colours were apparent everywhere. All this time music was playing, crowds cried Vive L'Empereur". Eugenie walked around the gardens enjoying the accolades, thrilled at the result. Metternich reported the cost of the fireworks alone was fr600,000, a light lunch at Montmartre, according to one diarist at that time, was just fr1.5.

Chapter Seven

A New City is Born

Napoleon and Haussmann.
Musée Carnavalet CCØ

One of Napoleon's major initiatives was the remodelling of Paris which began soon after the Empire was established and which he put into the hands of (Baron) Georges-Eugene Haussmann. He was the Regional Prefect and his remit was to bring light and air into the city and improve cross Paris travel. The wide boulevards are perhaps the most obvious feature, with the Rue de Rivoli completed in time for the World Fair in 1855.

This was a radical and wide ranging improvement and expansion of the suburbs. It also had the intention of removing the pockets of insurgency amongst the poor and nomadic population who had already shown their displeasure at his seizure of power. They lived in the labyrinth of dark, narrow streets with close packed buildings handy for constructing barricades a la "Les Miserables". Thousands were displaced and by opening up these areas it would allow the army access if necessary to quell any trouble.

The Imperial couple's trip to London in 1855 had resulted in a change in the city plans with Sydenham, perhaps for the only time in its history exerting its architectural muscle after their visit. The Crystal Palace with its signature iron and glass structure left a deep impression and on their return to Paris Eugenie took action. The plans for the new buildings in Les Halles, the principal food market were revised and the first stone pavilion pulled down. It was replaced with a Paxtonian style glass and iron complex which would house Les Halles for over a century and became one of the city landmarks. (It was demolished in the 1970's). Les Halles was just a 10 minute walk from the Tuileries so the Empress could and did keep an eye on the new plans and its progress.

Above all the massive programme of public works and modernisation was designed to create a new era of Imperial glory, the result was the economy boomed and the National debt grew. The rapidly increasing city population which stood at around two million had doubled in the preceding two decades so new water supplies, plus an extensive sewer system were constructed along with an expanded railway network in and around the capital with the new Gare du Nord as its high point, inaugurated in 1864.

Rows of neo-classical apartment buildings appeared, decorative and ornate features proliferated on both the new and old and from the rubble emerged grand department stores, hotels and pavement cafes. The shops would stay open till late and people of all classes would come out and enjoy the atmosphere and see and be seen, all illuminated by the end of the Empire by 50,000 gaslights. Parisians flaunted their wealth and spent accordingly. The new streets were filled with horses, carriages and served by a comprehensive omnibus service. There were parks and public squares and the Bois de Boulogne, a densely wooded area was developed to include two lakes, a zoo, an aquarium and the now famous Longchamp race course. New theatres, music halls and cabarets appeared. The architect of the opulent new Opera House, (of Phantom fame) was decided by a competition. Eugenie submitted her own plans worked up by the palace draughtsman which apparently resembled the town hall in Brescia. The commission went to Charles Garnier and the theatre is known as the Palais Garnier. It wasn't completed until after the Empire fell but by then it was already a landmark and incorporated some extravagant features, normally only found in a royal palace. It was the most expensive building of the Second Empire and is still active. The design puzzled the Empress and when asked to identify the style Garnier replied, "Napoleon 3rd".

The architects weren't afraid to borrow from the past as well as embracing the new, sometimes in the same building. The implementation of master plan wasn't straightforward but the city as we know it today was born in this period.

In the summer of 1861, during the early days of the American Civil War, Prince Napoleon was on a fact finding tour in the United States and on a stopover in Washington was invited to visit the White House and meet President Lincoln. When he arrived with the French Ambassador, he was surprised to find no one there to greet him, not even a doorman. They managed to get the attention of a passing official who let them in but the tour didn't get any better. After being introduced to the President and shaking hands they stood in silence whilst the chairs were rearranged before eventually sitting down but still nothing was said. With the party was Prince Napoleon's aide de camp, Lt-Colonel Camille Ferri Pisani who recorded the awkward events. The Prince, "impatient at being kept waiting took a cruel pleasure in remaining silent. Finally, the President took the risk of speaking of Prince Lucien, his father". Unfortunately, Lincoln had picked the wrong Bonaparte and when his aide pointed this out the President lost his confidence and the conversation descended into a few banal questions on the weather and the crossing. "The Prince still maintained his polite but cold front—as he customarily does when he does not care to help the conversation". Both parties must have been glad when the allotted time was up and Lincoln concluded the meeting with more handshaking.

They returned later that night for a state dinner but this time it was the President's wife that didn't impress the Prince. "Mrs. Lincoln was dressed in the French style without any taste; she has the manner of a petit bourgeois and wears tin jewellery."

In 1865 the Emperor went on another tour of Algeria leaving Eugenie as Regent. By now she felt more comfortable in the role and saw it as an effective way to promote some of her ideals, though many men had little regard for any woman in an influential position. They had far fewer rights in law as married women were regarded as legal minors and they weren't even allowed to wear trousers without a permit. From the outset Eugenie had developed a real sense of social purpose, much of her state allowance was given away, and she took over the leadership of the Société Maternelle, a charity established by Marie Antoinette to promote women's issues. She took an informed and active interest in the young, one trip to the Orphan Asylum in the notoriously volatile Faubourg Saint-Antoine, a very deprived area of the city was greeted with a hearty welcome. Her visit to a young person's prison resulted in a major change in conditions for all such institutions. She also paid regular visits to schools and hospitals, including those dealing with cholera victims. During severe outbreaks in Paris and Amiens in 1865/6 she went round the wards chatting to each patient seemingly without fear of catching the disease. Such charitable activities became a regular part of her life, generally lowkey early morning trips, in a plain carriage with just a single Lady in waiting. Most were unannounced which must have kept the officials on their toes. These visits weren't purely for show though she doesn't seem to have received much credit for her involvement.

Eugenie was an early feminist, acutely aware that women's education, especially at secondary level was severely lacking and worked with the Minister of Public Instruction, Victor Drury to create opportunities for young women. One such initiative in Paris saw 250-300 on every course held at the Sorbonne but these were middle class students and it didn't give them the important Baccalaureate, the pre university qualification. Paris lagged behind Lyon in this respect, where the first woman to pass those exams was in 1861.

Entry into the medical profession was notoriously difficult as it was viewed contrary to morals and social norms. The first woman to qualify was English, Elizabeth Garrett Anderson who had passed the requisite exams in Britain but wasn't allowed a medical licence, she then learnt French to make that final step. Madeline Bres was the first French female doctor to qualify in 1875.

When asked to approve the latest list of candidates for the prestigious Legion d'honneur Eugenie added the name of an artist called Rose Bonheur, making her the first woman to receive this award. To emphasise the point, she visited Bonheur in her studio to present it to her personally. She even went as far as nominating the popular writer and Republican, George Sand, (real name Aurore Dupin) to the Académie Française, the prestigious National Institution. In Eugenie's opinion "genius has no sex".

At the other end of social scale, she introduced a woman chef to the Tuileries, Marthe-Alice Pouypoudat. Whilst seeking shelter from a downpour at a Royal event near Biarritz, Eugenie was offered something to eat by this farmer's wife and a dish was created which became known as "Pain Farci en Croute Belle Crinoline". It consists of bread stuffed with a hot roulade of quail and Chaloose ham (which formed a sort of pate), drizzled with a salamis sauce and a local red Tursan wine. Madame Pouypoudat became friends with the Empress and eventually revealed her secret recipe to the palace chefs.

The Arts weren't an intellectual pursuit for the Empress. She understood the value of her patronage and commissioned many works but personally had a superficial appreciation of Art, she knew what she liked, whether it was regarded critically as good or bad. She did support the art scene with her purchases at the influential Salon exhibitions but her strengths lay in other directions, show her a relevant historical painting and she could explain all the political and military significance.

Napoleon was inherently conservative in his artistic choices but established the Salon des Refusés in 1863 where paintings rejected by the Academy of Fine Art were shown, so the works of artists such as Manet and Pissarro. The later salons became the home of the Impressionists though their art was seldom appreciated by visitors or critics alike.

Dramatic theatre didn't appeal to Eugenie no matter how well written and Opera was beyond her except for the light hearted Offenbach operettas. Attendance at the Opera was an important part of the social scene and another chance for all to show off but Napoleon wasn't keen. Whilst many thought he should be present as part of his duties as Emperor his appearances in the Royal Box were rare. Invariably once the performance began he would nod off pretty quickly and it needed a friendly tap on his shoulder from Eugenie's fan to wake him up. He'd then look round, smile at the audience and resume his nap.

If Eugenie wasn't attracted to the music, she certainly understood the star appeal of the world famous soprano Adelina Patti. Such was her prowess that Patti could earn more for one performance than the President of the US made in a year. Eugenie loved acting as matchmaker despite a poor track record and she encouraged Patti to marry the

Marquis de Caux, one of Napoleon's equerries. For a wedding present she gave the singer a comb decorated with 23 large diamonds.

Jewels were handed out with the same frequency as you would give away sweets.

Chapter Eight

Misadventure and Glory

As Paris prepared to host the World Fair in 1867, the intense political manoeuvring in Europe turned into war between two of their neighbours. Trouble across the continent had been brewing for years but it came to a head in 1866.

Into the equation had come the menacing figure of the Prussian Chancellor, Otto von Bismarck. Described years before as the "evil genius" he was well known in French court circles as he'd been Ambassador in Paris but his first visit to Biarritz in 1862 could have changed history for ever. He and his mistress went for a swim and were swept out by the current into dangerous waters. A lifeguard had to drag them to safety and both needed reviving on shore.

Count Otto Von Bismarck.
Musée Carnavalet CCØ

Imagine if he had drowned, how would Europe have evolved. Sadly, the poor lifeguard did drown a month later.

Rather strangely Bismarck's name became associated with high fashion. When brown unexpectedly came into vogue it was nicknamed Bismarck Brown. He may have been the most hated man in Europe but perversely Paris was a sea of brown, clothes, boots, hats, even sunshades, it was everywhere as rich and poor alike could afford clothes made in that colour. The fashion might appear dull and dreary but the man himself was anything but and he was determined to shake up Europe and unify Germany under Prussia.

Bismarck's first step meant separating a group of northern states from Austrian control. The war lasted just seven weeks and was a swift and decisive victory for Prussia. Johann Strauss then composed the Blue Danube waltz to cheer up the Austrians after the defeat.

That war had come when Napoleon was embroiled in a disastrous plan to create a new pro French regime in Mexico as part of his colonial ambitions. Napoleon had persuaded the Austrian Archduke Maximilian to become Emperor there in 1864 and promised French support. The whole venture was short lived, the French army under repeated attack by rebels and depleted by disease was withdrawn as tensions rose at home, and the regime collapsed. In June 1867 Maximilian was executed (as depicted in a Manet painting) and his wife Charlotte, who had come to Europe to try and persuade Napoleon to change his mind suffered a major breakdown. It's not clear if she ever understood what had happened and her final five decades were spent hidden away, mostly in her native Belgium.

Opinion is divided as to how influential Eugenie was in the Mexican project, she was certainly fervent in her support of the Catholic state and concerned about the spread of Protestantism from North America. She would undoubtedly have expressed her opinion but the plan had been conjured up by the Emperor himself and it proved increasingly unpopular. At the same time, he had an army in Rome, protecting Papal territory from Italian Nationalists, another long term and problematic commitment.

Despite the events in Mexico, the seven month long Exposition Universelle was a spectacular distraction with over 50,000 exhibitors and more than nine million visitors and as importantly it showed off the new Paris to the many Emperors, Kings and Princes who attended. Queen Victoria wasn't amongst them, she was in mourning following

Prince Albert's death but Eugenie sailed over to Osborne to try and persuade her to change her mind but to no avail.

With so many heads of state in town security was tight but there was an assassination attempt on the Russian Tsar, Alexander II whilst he was travelling with Napoleon. The Emperor attempted to calm his visitor's fears claiming it was most likely directed towards him. I doubt Alexander believed him since he was regularly targeted and did eventually die from an assassin's bomb in 1881.

Victor Hugo wrote a guide to the Fair even though he'd been exiled on Jersey and Guernsey during the Empire. A fierce opponent of Napoleon, he'd published numerous articles criticising "Napoleon le Petit" as he called him, though his most famous publication in this era was "Les Miserables".

Some suggest the World Fair was the high point of the Empire but there was one more glory to celebrate, the completion of the Suez Canal. Here Eugenie was definitely influential as it was in the hands of her cousin, the French diplomat, Ferdinand des Lessops. Bonaparte had contemplated a similar idea years before but Nelson put paid to his ambitions in the area.

De Lessops obtained the building and operating concessions from the Egyptian head of state, the Khedive in 1854 and 6 and the plan was for the Canal to link the Mediterranean with the Red Sea which would provide a short cut to India and beyond. The British made it clear early on that they were unhappy with the project as they regarded it as a great threat to their trade and rule in the Indian subcontinent plus there were serious doubts the Canal would be built. Consequently, Napoleon was initially wary of offering public support even though much of the private finance would come from French banks and shareholders. Eugenie had continually acted as a powerful intermediary when the numerous problems and doubts arose, De Lessops called her the Canal's guardian angel. It was probably the only time she and Prince Napoleon saw eye to eye but it wasn't until around 1864 that the Emperor began to actively promote the enterprise.

The building operation was massive with the initial digging done with just picks and shovels. It's estimated more than 1.5 million workers were involved at some stage but controversially many were forced labour. Thousands died from disease and the project encountered many difficulties but in November 1869 the 102 mile long Canal was ready to open. It cut 4,000 miles off the usual route from Britain to India round the Cape of Good Hope.

Throughout this period Napoleon's health was deteriorating, it was poor at the start of his reign and his lifestyle was hardly conducive to healthy living. He'd been suffering from bladder stones diagnosed in 1865 which was compounded by his rheumatoid arthritis and gout but he hated doctors and all the while was trying to keep the severity of his illness from everyone including his wife. At the same time his plan to liberalise the regime had only resulted in more unrest and poor Eugenie was facing open hostility from both her enemies and those supposed friends. One of the leaders of the character assassination was Princess Mathilde who, in briefing the Goncourt brothers the influential chroniclers of the period, portrayed Eugenie as useless, self-centred, uncaring, narcissistic, immodest and above all not French! Given her status the remarks spread like wildfire.

There was no possibility that the Imperial couple could go to Egypt together so Eugenie was dispatched to open the Canal by herself. She had contemplated tacking on a trip to India but then decided she would be away too long. It was a relief for her to escape Paris and having admired the Egyptian exhibits at the World Fair she was looking forward to seeing the country.

Meanwhile Napoleon recovered a little of his vigour, the British Ambassador observed he was "consoling himself for her absence by giving small dances at the Tuileries for some young American ladies".

Eugenie reputedly ordered 250 dresses from Worth for the trip and relied on her packer and luggage maker, Louis Vuitton to ensure they arrived in good condition. Vuitton had been working for her since her marriage and his invention of flat topped cases made stacking much easier than the previous domed lid models.

Eugenie left France on September 30th 1869 accompanied by a party of 40, including her Dentist, Dr Thomas Evans who would feature more prominently less than a year later. She was probably the most recognisable woman in the world and France was at its zenith.

Her first stop was Venice which greeted her with a carnival style welcome, serenaded by 100 singers on the Grand Canal. It was then on to Athens and a Royal inspection of the Acropolis but she had no appreciation of the "wretched ruins" and thought it all depressing so breezed through, barely glancing at the ancient monuments. It was a different story in Constantinople (Istanbul) where the whole fleet was paraded in celebration. On the evening of her arrival the Sultan's barge, manned by forty oarsmen, ferried Eugénie across the illuminated Bosphorus to an 11 course banquet in the Palace. It was estimated that half a million people were watching, either from the shore or at sea. The Sultan, Abdul Aziz, who by all accounts had fallen for her in Paris was perhaps a little over eager to impress and showed her round his harem. His mother seeing him strolling arm-in-arm with an unveiled and unknown woman gave the Empress a fierce punch in the stomach that almost knocked her down. An International incident was avoided and whilst mother and son argued, everyone else burst out laughing. As a parting gift the Sultan gave her a rather creepy carpet with an embroidered portrait of Napoleon, complete with real human hair and a moustache.

The Imperial yacht, l'Aigle (Eagle) reached Alexandria on November 5th well ahead of the opening. The Khedive, keen to make sure there wouldn't be any trouble had made a pre-emptive strike on the criminal fraternity by arresting 97 of the city's most violent offenders who were then dumped at sea in sacks weighted down with stones. Eugenie's party had time to go down to Cairo by train which was illuminated in her honour and she attended an Egyptian wedding, incognita, in Arab dress. A trip down the Nile and a visit to the Pyramids guided by an eminent French archaeologist impressed the Empress on what was her first genuine holiday for some time. She was still receiving news updates from Napoleon in Paris amongst them this rather sweet message "you have seen the pyramids and the forty centuries have beheld you; we embrace you tenderly".

She arrived in Port Said early on the morning of November 16th to be greeted by her cousin and was accommodated in opulent new apartments in the Gezirah Palace. The Khedive had been to the World Fair and had ordered these to resemble those at Versailles. He'd also had the road built from Cairo to Giza for her visit to the pyramids. He was another of her platonic conquests.

The night before the opening a British naval survey vessel HMS Newport had sneakily manoeuvred herself, in the dark, through the numerous waiting ships to the front of the queue ahead of the Imperial yacht. Strangely this was omitted from official French reports. The British captain was officially reprimanded but unofficially received a vote of thanks from the Admiralty for his actions in promoting British interests and for demonstrating such superb seamanship!

The Opening and Blessing of the Suez Canal November 17th 1869. LOC

At 8am the following morning after the ceremonial opening the official flotilla and a total of around 120 ships entered the canal, as Eugenie recalled. "The sight was one of such magnificence and proclaimed the grandeur of the French Empire so eloquently that I could scarcely control myself – I rejoiced, triumphantly. The frightful nightmare I had brought with me from Paris suddenly vanished, as if at the touch of some magic ring. For the last time I was convinced that a wonderful future lay in store for my son, and I prayed to God that He would help me with the crushing burden which I might soon have to shoulder if the Emperor's health showed no improvement".

There was plenty of entertainment on the banks as they made their progress, Arab horseman showed off their equestrian tricks, whirling devishes (a religious sect known for their wild dancing rituals) held hot coals in their mouth and swallowed live scorpions and an acrobat walked across a tightrope complete with two babies strapped to his ankles. During the excitement one of the Imperial party went walkabout, her pet turtle, La Reine and it ended its days in Cairo Zoo.

More seriously there was genuine fear some vessels might run aground as it was only 25 feet deep in places. Fortunately, all went to plan but the Canal wasn't completely finished for several years.

The inaugural day finished with a celebratory dinner. The Khedive had imported gilt chairs and marble topped tables from Paris and recruited 1,000 livered footmen and 500 chefs from all over France to service his 6,000 guests. He wanted to premiere a new opera by Giuseppe Verdi but the composer said he was too busy so the new opera house staged a performance of another of his works, Rigoletto. The Khedive didn't give up and eventually Verdi agreed and his most famous opera Aida, set in Egypt, was premiered in Cairo two years later.

At midnight Eugenie, accompanied by the Emperor Franz Joseph and the Khedive, arrived at the banquet. Dressed in a diamond studded dress with a spectacular diamond tiara she shone like a star for all to admire. As they toasted the Canal with champagne did she wonder what was in store for her and the Empire. As it turned out this was her last headline act on the world stage.

Chapter Nine

The End is Nigh

Eugenie returned to find neither the political situation nor Napoleon's health had improved. The new head of the council of ministers insisted that Eugenie should no longer be allowed to attend their meetings. In part this was to protect her from being blamed for influencing any decisions and as importantly so they could distance themselves from her unpopularity.

In May Napoleon won an unexpectedly overwhelming victory in a plebiscite over the new liberal laws and celebrated with a ball at the Tuileries. Surely the Emperor was safe but whilst the internal opposition was kept at bay, Bismarck was eying up the options as he plotted the final steps for German unification. He'd seen off Austria, and France who shared a border with several German states was next on his list and it was clear it wouldn't take much to inflame the already uneasy situation. His calculated assessment of Napoleon was chilling, "overrated in intellect and underrated in heart". Ironically, he was far more impressed by the Empress "The only man in Paris".

The catalyst for war was Bismarck's offer of a German candidate to become the new King of Spain. France was outraged as they saw it as meddling in European affairs that were none of their business. Suddenly the situation escalated totally out of hand as the country appeared set on teaching Prussia a lesson, the senior Generals promised a speedy victory but it was a ridiculously bullish and unfounded assessment. All through this period just when France needed Napoleon to be at his best, he was suffering from debilitating attacks of pain exacerbated by the indecision of the doctors over the best course of treatment. Periodically dosed up with laudanum that also impacted his decision making. One modern medical paper thought it a prime example of the "influence the bad health of a sovereign can exercise on the destiny of his country".

Although Bismarck withdrew the German candidacy France went further and demanded a commitment that they wouldn't try again. A meeting between their Ambassador and the King of Prussia didn't resolve the issue but Bismarck's carefully edited version of events published in the infamous Ems telegram was, as he himself noted, a "red rag to the Gallic bull" and pushed the Emperor into declaring war on the 19th July.

Napoleon and Prince Imperial at the army base at Chalons.
Musée Carnavalet   CCØ

The trap was set and Bismarck knew victory would mean he could complete unification without external interference. The French troops were cheered on their way with cries of "To Berlin", amidst an air of excitement and invincibility but all too soon it turned into desperation and defeat.

At some stage Eugenie gathered some personal mementoes and documents and had them shipped out of the country.

Napoleon was to lead the army though he could barely sit on a horse and even the shaking of a carriage was painful. He looked and felt dreadful and even at his best his military acumen wasn't a patch on his famous uncle. On 28th July he caught the train to the army HQ. Eugenie's concern for her husband was mirrored, probably intensified for her son as the 14 year old Prince Imperial had gone to war with his father and although not directly in the front line came close enough to hear the cannonballs thud into the ground and pick up a bullet that dropped nearby. Eugenie was once more Regent but still not allowed to attend the ministerial meetings. The messages from the front started to arrive and it was immediately evident how wrong the generals were, the Prussians were a far superior army, better equipped, trained and organised. Napoleon's telegrams made distressing reading "nothing is ready: our troops are insufficient; in my opinion we are already lost" a string of defeats followed as did the desperate telegrams "Terrible disaster, total defeat".

Eugenie didn't shirk her duties and as it went from bad to worse summoned the council of ministers to the Tuileries. They advised her to recall the Emperor, she refused, anticipating further disaster at home if he returned. It was now becoming more dangerous for her and in desperation she asked the Austrian Ambassador's wife to look after her personal and valuable jewellery. The Crown Jewels had been handed to the Treasury, she'd even taken the precaution of getting a receipt before they were sent to the port city of Brest for safe keeping. Perhaps she sensed her personal gems could be a useful source of funds if worse was to come. Two of her ladies in waiting arrived at the Metternichs and tearfully produced the jewels as Princess Pauline recounted in her memoirs "some of the cases were missing, and all these diamonds and pearls and countless precious stones were merely wrapped in newspaper". They were sent with an attaché in a diplomatic bag to London, (these "bags" which could be everything from briefcases to boxes couldn't be searched by police and customs and were used for private communications from diplomats to their home country or colleagues abroad). At first the Bank of England refused to accept the jewellery, fortunately the Austrian Ambassador persuaded them to change their mind. At the same time Eugenie ordered the most important art works in St Cloud and the Louvre to be removed for safety.

Weeks later when the blame game started Eugenie found herself named as the instigator of the war. True she was in favour but her feelings were in line with the rest of the country. She hadn't been allowed at the council meetings so couldn't have been party to the ultimate decision but she supposedly turned on the ailing Napoleon and pressured him into action, rather like Lady Macbeth "Screw your courage to the sticking place, and we'll not fail". It's claimed Eugenie used the phrase "My War", which she denied, but the term appeared in the magazine, "La Volonte Nationale", the mouthpiece of Prince Napoleon, and it stuck. She was to live out her life as the scapegoat.

The Emperor's fate was sealed at the Battle of Sedan, in North East France. Vastly outnumbered the odds were against the French from the start. Napoleon racked by pain, perhaps wished for a glorious death in battle, he tried his best to be killed out of a vain hope it would somehow save the Empire but instead he was forced into a humiliating surrender on September 2nd.

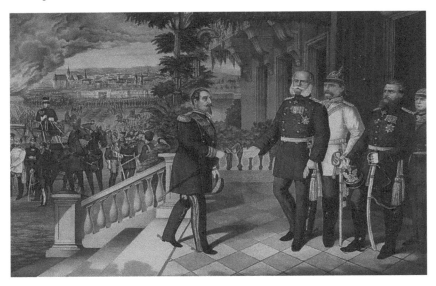

Napoleon surrenders to Kaiser William I. LOC

When the first news reached Paris Eugenie refused to believe it, but it was followed by a telegram from Napoleon himself. She fainted and on recovering launched into a torrent of recrimination and anger directed towards her husband. What followed over the next two days were a series of meetings without resolution as those around her deserted the Palace.

As the crowds began to assemble outside the Tuileries on the morning of the 4th she gave Napoleon's treasured Charlemagne Talisman to a trusted servant to hide, which he did in his kitchen cupboard and then pasted over the doors with a map of France. By early afternoon it was only too evident she had to leave. Uppermost must have been the thought of the fate of Marie Antoinette and now she faced the personal risk of being lynched by the howling mob already banging on the door. Some thought she'd already left it too late to escape but her only comfort was news that the Prince Imperial was on his way to Belgium.

Dressed in a simple black dress, a thin waterproof cloak and black hat with veil she just had time to pick up a very small handbag continuing nothing more than a couple of handkerchiefs. She embraced the small group of friends still with her and accompanied by Prince Metternich and the Italian ambassador Count Nigra, who both urged her to hurry, fled the Palace. She did have one lady willing to join her, a lowly placed member of her entourage, her second reader, Madame Lebreton. They couldn't go through the front entrance, the mob were already pulling down the Imperial Eagles, the only option was through the Louvre which adjoined the Tuileries. The problem was the door was locked but just in time the state treasurer arrived with his set of keys and they hurried through the bare galleries. As they reached the side doors, they heard the cries of "Death to the Spaniard", it must have sent a shiver down her spine. Nearby was a cab, but one street urchin recognised the Empress and called out, Nigra rushed over to silence him, fortunately the cry couldn't be heard above the din.

An understated version of the escape. Musée Carnavalet CCØ

The Empress and Madame Lebreton were pushed into it the cab. They tried a couple of addresses but no one opened the doors and out of desperation arrived at the home of the Imperial dentist, an American called Dr Thomas Evans. They were admitted to a room without disclosing their identities. Evans, who had been out in the city with his nephew Dr Crane was aware of the disturbances and on his return was pointed in the direction of the two veiled women waiting upstairs for him. Evans immediately agreed to help, that was the easy part, he decided Eugenie would be presented as an English invalid and her companion. Crane and Evans did a little late night reconnaissance and at 5am the following morning the four left in Evans' carriage, with Crane at the reigns. They safely negotiated the guards at the city gates and then drove for 24 hours, going north up the Route Imperial and changing carriages and horses several times. These were a mixed bunch but Evans was a slick talker and with a bit of subterfuge and hard cash managed to get what was needed without rousing suspicions. Eugenie would stay in the carriage well out of sight eating whatever meagre rations they could bring her. Forced to stop for one night in a dismal hotel at la Rivière the only option for the next stage was the train, much riskier. Eugenie noted they had to cross some fields by foot on their way to the Station. There she was frightened as one of staff seemed to recognise her, but it was just one stop to Lisieux, and safely negotiated. It was raining heavily and as Evans went in search of a carriage a bedraggled Eugenie huddled in the doorway. It was a long wait but he managed to hire another carriage to take them to Deauville where Mrs Evans was holidaying. They were smuggled into her room via the garden, much to his wife's surprise.

They probably thought every police agent in the country was on the alert but Evans avoided the few locals who seemed interested in the politics and the papers made no mention of the missing Empress. Luck had favoured them so far but now they needed to find a boat to take them to England. Evans and Crane went down to the harbour and the best option was a yacht, the Gazelle, owned by a British baronet Sir John Burgoyne, a distinguished ex-soldier. When told of their mission he declined to get involved even though he was due to sail the following morning. He must have realised the political ramifications. Evans called on his honour but Bourgogne countered saying the weather forecast was pretty dire and he wasn't sure they would go anyway, but after consulting his wife they agreed. As he prepared for the voyage two mysterious men asked to look over the yacht which they did, who knows who they were. Fortunately, the passengers were still in the hotel.

After supper, a little before midnight they made their way along a muddy path to the boat and at 7am when the tide was right they set sail. Crane said his goodbyes and returned to Paris, what stories he would have to tell when all were safe. Initially the Gazelle made good progress but then the wind changed and started to blow hard and the yacht sustained some meaningful damage. The sensible option was to seek refuge in a French port, instead they ploughed on. Eugenie, who seemed impervious to the conditions was possibly the coolest head aboard. The gale intensified, it was madness, Madame Lebreton had long since sunk to her knees and resorted to prayer. Around 6pm they tantalisingly spotted land but they couldn't reach it as the waves swept over and into the rolling boat, forming an impenetrable barrier and almost battering them into submission. The thunder, lightning and torrential rain was relentless, had they sunk now no one would know what had become of them but gradually around midnight the gale eased and they dropped anchor at Ryde on the Isle of Wight. It was 4am, a journey of 110 miles on a normal crow flying day had taken 21 hours in the worst conditions the Channel could offer so they opened some champagne to celebrate. One of Sir John's relatives, Hugh Bourgogne, a naval commander fared far worse that day, his ship HMS Captain sank off the Spanish coast with a loss of 500 lives.

The party went in search of a hotel but their first choice didn't want anything to do with such a motley crew. When they did find refuge at the York Hotel it was nothing special but it was dry and it was in England. When Evans met up with the Empress later than morning, he could show her the headlines indicating the Prince Imperial was also now on English soil and only a few hours later they set off to Hastings to meet him.

Almost immediately Burgoyne wrote to the Foreign Secretary Lord Granville and the Queen's personal secretary Colonel Ponsonby explaining his accidental involvement, he certainly wasn't the embodiment of the Scarlet Pimpernel and was conscious his actions would be regarded as totally inappropriate. Granville had little sympathy for the Empress, as he thought she'd brought it on herself by meddling in French foreign policy.

What of the two people who had joined the Empress, they certainly weren't walk on parts.

Thomas Wiltberger Evans (1823-97) was born in Philadelphia to a Quaker family. As a young man he was good with his hands but although his family tried to persuade him from a career as a "tooth puller" Evans proved to be a pioneer in this field. A chance meeting with a retired physician who saw one of his demonstrations in Philadelphia and who was living in Paris resulted in his move to France. Evans took with him new techniques to Europe including the use of Nitros oxide, as an anaesthetic and amalgam and gold fillings which would become standard and proved popular with those who could afford his services and who he chose to treat. He established an impressive upper class client base not only the Imperial Family but other heads of state consulted him as did the wealthy and influential. He made his millions through what would now be called insider dealing during the redevelopment of Paris (his estate was valued conservatively at more than $110 million dollars in 2022 terms). His waiting room was also a very convenient meeting place for off the record meetings between the influential elites and heads of state would summon the dentist to relay messages relying on his own personal discretion. Despite his links to the Second Empire his career was unaffected and "Handsome Tom" became a major patron of the arts in the Third Republic. He left the bulk of his estate to found a dental school and museum in Philadelphia.

Madame Adelaide Lebreton-Bourkabi, (1817-1899) was the sister of General Bourkabi, a decorated army commander who fought in both the Crimean and Franco Prussian wars.

She'd grown up as a playmate of the daughters of King Louis Philippe and had become the second reader to the Empress in 1867 and like Evans had been part of her entourage to the opening of the Suez Canal. A reader would be required, as the name suggests, to read to the Empress, however Eugenie preferred to do this herself so Lebreton's duties would usually be to write a few letters on her behalf and stay until the official Ladies in waiting arrived. After her first husband died, she'd married a court physician but was separated so was free to go with the Empress as she made her escape. I can't imagine she had any idea how her future would unfold but she remained with Eugenie until her death at Farnborough Hill.

The Empress met up with her son at the Marine hotel in Hastings, where they stayed for two weeks. Their accommodation wasn't very comfortable and it felt like living in a goldfish bowl surrounded by the inquisitive locals though the Mayor agreed not to advertise their presence to keep voyeurs to a minimum. By the end of the month, they'd moved to far better lodgings at Camden Place in Kent. (Now the Chislehurst golf club.)

Chapter Ten

In Exile

Camden Place, Chislehurst

Sources diverge on how they came to live in Chislehurst. Evans said that he found it by accident, others that it was one of many offers the Empress received but more convincingly was the fact the owner, a solicitor/financier called Nathaniel Strode was the trustee of estates for Napoleon's former mistress, Lizzie Howard and he'd previously been paid 900,000 francs from the Emperor's civil list. Napoleon had visited the property whilst in exile and for a short time had been engaged to the daughter of the house until his roving eye had put an end to that relationship. Strode had bought the house in 1860 and set about rebuilding it in the French style, adding two wings and filling it with various souvenirs from the Paris Exposition of 1867 including Iron gates which were added to the entrance to the park. Whether he was a real Francophile or just an opportunist isn't clear but Evans who had been scouting properties in Torquay was perhaps tipped off about the Strode connection.

News of the escape to England brought a stream of French exiles to the area and some former members of her staff found their way to Camden Place. Amongst them was her cook which was a relief to the Empress who hadn't appreciated the seaside cuisine. Eugenie received many visitors during this period including Prince Napoleon (Plon Plon) who was a great irritation and Princess Metternich her close friend in Paris. Her main concern was political, as the Austrians had seemingly been warned about some compromising papers in the Emperor's possession that indicated a deal had been done to help the French if they went to war with Prussia. The papers mysteriously vanished from his bureau shortly afterwards and the Metternichs and Eugenie never met again. Many in France wanted those documents to disappear too!

On October 30th she travelled through Belgium to visit Napoleon in his prison at Wilhelmshöhe near Kassel in Northern Germany. Although she'd written endearingly to Napoleon, in sharp contrast to her outburst after Sedan he greeted her rather coldly which came as a surprise. In private it was a more emotional reunion and she stayed there for a couple of days whilst they discussed tactics. The Emperor sold his small estate near Rome with half the money going to Chislehurst and the rest was sent via Dr Evans to help his imprisoned soldiers suffering in captivity. The French had been hit by a smallpox epidemic which killed at least 25,000 men with around four times that number infected. The Prussian Army had been vaccinated but not the population as a whole and around 160,000 German civilians died of the disease spread by French prisoners of war.

Wilhelmshöhe had been used by Napoleon's uncle Jerome when he ruled as King of Westphalia and had nicknamed it Napoleonshöhe and there was still a portrait of Napoleon's mother, Queen Hortense in the Palace. The Emperor had with him several longstanding members of his staff and that essential extra, his hairdresser. With a gentlemanly

Governor it had the feel of a luxury health resort and Napoleon's condition improved significantly. The Prussians weren't being totally altruistic, the bill for their stay was later sent to the French Government.

Their British counterparts were looking on with some concern as they wanted to stay neutral. The Queen had a foot in both camps, personal friendship and family ties. She'd sent a sympathetic letter almost immediately Eugenie had arrived and on November 30th made a private visit with her daughter Princess Beatrice describing it as a sad visit, like a strange dream. Given one of her other daughters, Vicky was married to the German Crown Prince and future Kaiser, the Anglo French German triangle pulled in many different directions. No doubt Victoria was keen to find out what had gone on in Kassel and relay the details to her ministers. Vicky later offered to send her mother part of a screen from Eugenie's private rooms at St Cloud which had been liberated by a Prussian soldier. This, she thought could then be passed on to Eugenie at a suitable time. The British vetoed the seemingly innocuous idea as just too political.

Surprisingly perhaps the war hadn't ended with Sedan. A provisional French government was established which later morphed into the Third Republic but their primary concern was dealing with the Prussian advance on Paris. They laid siege to the capital from September 19th for four months, St Cloud was destroyed but it needed some heavy shelling before the city fell. The galleries of the Tuileries were converted into hospital wards to cope with the sick and wounded.

This was a period of great hardship for the Parisians and at one stage food was so short they ate the zoo animals including their famous elephants Castor and Pollux.

With normal communications impossible the French resorted to sending out messages via hot air balloons, 67 left the city, mostly at night carrying mail and homing pigeons. The birds returned with messages, eventually using an early form of microfilm which was then transcribed. Inevitably some of the pigeons were shot for food so never made it back.

The new German Empire was proclaimed on January 18th in the Hall of Mirrors in Versailles to emphasise their supremacy and the armistice was signed 10 days later. 30,000 German troops subsequently staged a victory parade through the city, not for the last time in history. Britain and the US sent substantial food aid to the beleaguered population and a final Peace treaty was signed on May 10th. The settlement included territorial gains with Alsace Lorraine being absorbed into the new Germany. In fewer than 100 years the new country had gone from 300 separate German speaking entities to one state.

The French capital had meanwhile descended into more bloody conflict as soldiers of the National Guard had seized power in March and formed the Paris Commune. Tens of thousands were estimated to have been killed between the rival forces. The Commune's revolutionary socialist ideas are said to have influenced the theories of Marx and Engels but the regime only lasted a couple of months so little was achieved except the symbolic burning down of the Tuileries.

Ruins of the interior of the Tuileries destroyed in May 1871
Musée Carnavalet CCØ

The government eventually decided to demolish the substantial remains of the Palace which had stood untouched, except by nature. When the site was cleared in 1883 bits and pieces were sold off as souvenirs and Charles Frederick Worth took full advantage. The following weeks large parts of the building including columns, statuary and whole sections of the façade complete with windows and a balcony were transported to his house where they were fashioned into decorative garden features. It's almost certain several items including a pair of doors in the main hall of Farnborough Hill decorated with the Napoleonic bee came from his scavenging.

Throughout this early period of exile Eugenie was vilified in the French press, censorship had been eased and she bore the brunt of some vindictive reporting and vicious, often pornographic caricatures which left a permanent scar on her reputation.

Napoleon was released on March 19th and was greeted by the Mayor and thousands of well-wishers at Dover. Ironically family members of the former King, Louis Philippe were returning to France from exile and they met near the Station. Eugenie curtsied and the men merely raised their hats as they walked past.

A week later the Imperial family were invited to Windsor on a private visit and the crowds came out to cheer. By custom they reciprocated the invitation and Victoria travelled to Chislehurst, she did however complain in her diary about the overheated rooms. Napoleon liked the heating on full blast, Eugenie preferred fresh air and Victoria loved the cold. These visits were a problem for the French government as they saw this as recognition of Napoleon as still "Emperor of the French" (and that's how he recorded his status in the census a few days later). British officials had stayed clear of making any public acknowledgment of their presence in the country and assurances that they showed no favour were met with disbelief in Paris. The first meeting between anyone in the government and Napoleon was accidental when the

Prime Minister, William Gladstone, visiting some friends in the area "bumped" into him on the station platform.

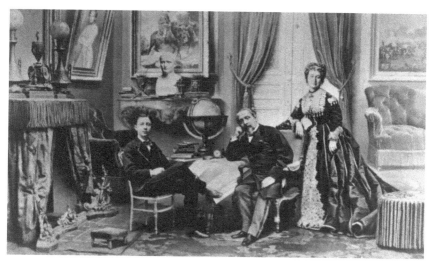

The Family Reunited. ©Photo 12/Alamy Stock Photo

Napoleon began to settle into a very gentlemanly existence, as he knew only too well from the Orsini affair it was a country with a pretty liberal attitude to asylum seekers. He could have opted to live in his mother's family Chateau at Arenenberg in Switzerland, which had been bought back as a present by Eugenie for her husband but the freedom that Britain allowed them and their experiences of life and friendships made it more acceptable to stay in Kent. It was also close to France should he consider trying to force a revolt and be restored to power, after all he'd used Britain as a springboard for such an action before. The government fervently hoped he wouldn't but he had other ideas.

Camden Place was obviously considerably smaller than any of their other residences and in the 1871 census taken on April 2nd it recorded the main household consisted of 32 people, including numerous, mainly French servants. It included triplets who had previously been taken into service as pages. Nearby in a growing enclave were many more French refugees who serviced the Imperial family. There were a few others with ulterior motives, as French spies were frequently to be seen nearby, one had a telescope in the windmill on Chislehurst Common, others stationed themselves in the trees overlooking the property, all reporting back to Paris on the comings and goings. Quite why they were so obvious isn't reported!

In September a world weary Eugenie went to see her mother in Madrid and Napoleon and the Prince Imperial trundled off to Torquay where they were warmly welcomed. The spies followed, wondering if they'd found an unlikely hotbed of French Imperialism.

Many of the exiles arriving at Camden Place wished for an audience with the Emperor who felt obliged to see them. Crowds travelled down from London by the train load to attend the Sunday church services to ogle at them. One unexpected consequence of the influx of French emigres was an increased demand for violets, the Bonaparte flower. It's said the great Napoleon picked some violets in the gardens of Fontainebleau shortly before he was sent into exile on Elba and decided it would become his symbol. From then on his admirers would wear them to show they supported the Bonaparte cause. The tradition continued well beyond the Second Empire and her couturier, Worth would send Eugenie a bunch of violets every year on her birthday.

Several wardrobes full of her clothes had been rescued from the Tuileries in the hours after her escape and other items were bought at sales by her representatives and sent on to Kent. With few funds at hand some of her jewels safely kept in the Bank of England now needed to be sold.

Her favourites stones were pearls, diamonds and emeralds. Green was the Bonaparte colour so she was definitely on message. One amazing diamond belt displayed at the 1855 World Fair had 4,485 diamonds, it was later redesigned and divided into smaller pieces.

The first sales in 1871 were private transactions including pearls to a wealthy German industrialist, Count Henckel von Donnersmarck.

Selling to the enemy must have been galling especially as he was an ardent Bismarck supporter. He'd been living in Paris when war broke out and one of Eugenie's early acts as Regent was to order the seizure of all his papers.

The Eugenie diamond, once the property of Catherine the Great of Russia was sold to Malhār Rāo, the ruler of Baroda in India for £12,000, it's now worth many millions.

In 1872 there were two auctions, the first was through Henry Emmanuel of New Bond Street, a noted diamond expert. It was advertised in the New York Times and no doubt attracted some wealthy Americans. The advert made great show of the pathos attached to the sale "A lady parting with her jewels is a hard fact which is unmistakable, and it is possible that the popular sympathy will be more deeply roused than at any event in the Imperial history since the flight from Paris and the surrender at Sedan". The extensive collection included the present from Napoleon of a diadem worn on semi state occasions, numerous gifts from visiting heads of state and many other luxury items. Several pieces had appeared in portraits of her over the years including a cross which had featured in a notable painting by Winterhalter. Of special significance was a necklace of black olive shaped matched pearls and a pendant with numerous diamonds and pearls which she had worn with the Crown Jewels. There were more necklaces plus brooches and bangles featuring diamonds, sapphires and rubies and a special diamond encrusted gold watch. The basic monetary value was estimated to be worth between £60-80,000 around £6-8 million today but given the provenance would normally be expected to fetch much more.

The second sale was through Christie's in June and featured 123 lots including many more emeralds and consisted largely of brooches, bracelets, earrings, hairpins, necklaces, a few tiaras and other fashionable pieces.

Not all her Jewels were offered for sale, some would be given as presents in future years and pieces regularly come up for auction.

One diamond and sapphire feather brooch was a wedding present to Queen Mary and may still be in the Royal Collection.

Photo PD David Liuzz

The gold Empress Crown was restored to Eugenie early in her exile. Made for the 1855 World Fair it featured 2490 diamonds and 56 emeralds. It was left in her will to Princess Marie Clotilde Bonaparte.

It resurfaced at auction in 1988 and the buyer donated it to the Louvre.

The most famous single jewel was the Regent diamond, the second largest in the world and part of the Crown Jewels hidden away during the war. Worn by Marie Antoinette on her hat, it later appeared embedded in the hilt of Napoleon Bonaparte's ceremonial sword. Napoleon lll had it reset for Eugenie in a Greek style diadem. It wasn't put up for auction in the great sale of 1887, when most of the important and valuable Crown Jewels were auctioned off by the French Government at way below market value in a symbolic severance from past monarchical regimes. The 141 carat stone was retained and is in the Louvre, valued today (2022) at about £50 million.

Whilst on the surface Napoleon III was living a pleasant retirement, watching local cricket matches, walking round the town and attending a variety of events as a VIP, he was covertly planning a return to power. The main obstacle was his health, which hadn't been improved by the foggy days and nights of Kent which adversely affected his rheumatism. In September 1872 his bladder stone attacks started up again and his attempts to prove his fitness by riding a horse were agony. He eventually called in the doctors and their solution was an operation, which they agreed should have been done years before. Whilst Eugenie was worried about his health there's no sense anyone thought it would be fatal but the stone was bigger than the doctors expected, the size of a small bird's egg and after two very painful procedures and with a third about to begin his condition suddenly deteriorated and on the morning of January 9th 1873 he died. Eugenie was distraught.

In his will he begged forgiveness from his wife, "I hope that my memory will be dear to her and that when I am dead, she will forgive me whatever sorrows I may have caused her". In fact their relationship at Camden Place had been pretty harmonious. Thousands queued to attend the lying in state but Eugenie was too upset to attend the funeral itself at the nearby St. Mary's Catholic Church. It's estimated it attracted a crowd of more than 17,000 with the mourners including most of the famous names from the Second Empire and the French army. The Prince of Wales represented the Queen, and as the Prince Imperial, who'd led the cortège left the church there were cries of "Vive L'Empéreur! Vive Napoléon IV!"

Almost immediately Prince Napoleon suggested he should come back with him to be educated properly. You can probably guess their response.

Chapter Eleven

The Prince Imperial

Prince Imperial c1875. Downey.
Musée Carnavalet CCØ

Louis had been trained to succeed his father from birth. He'd been given his first uniform as a member of the Imperial Guard at the age of nine months and put on a horse before he was two. He would regularly accompany his father to Military reviews dressed in original Bonaparte style uniforms and his bedtime stories would feature tales of his distinguished ancestor's glorious victories.

When he was three he was given a large model railway in the private park at St Cloud. The figure of eight track ran up hills, over viaducts and bridges and came complete with a small station and a windup engine. Next to the track was a small tent where he could sit and play. For his 7th birthday his present was a large model frigate built by the Navy workshops which he would sail on the carp pond at Fontainebleau aided by navigation lessons from the Naval chief.

His devoted nurse was Miss Shaw who'd been recommended by Queen Victoria and had the added bonus of helping him learn English. There's little doubt he was doted on by his parents but very spoilt by his father, his mother was stricter but Napoleon would often let him play in his study, making paper animals out of state documents and generally behave without limits or punishments. His real training began at 13 but was halted a year later when he went to war. After he settled at Camden Place his old tutor moved nearby but it was decided in 1872 that he would go to military college at Woolwich.

He was a charming, lively, good looking young man and a favourite of Queen Victoria. Unintimidated by her, Louis would regularly sit next to her when invited over for lunch or dinner which was a boon for the other guests. Victoria was infamous for the speed at which she ate and when she finished a course all the plates were cleared regardless of whether the other diners had done the same. Louis would chat to her during the meal which gave everyone else a chance to eat without risking indigestion or struggling to manage more than a morsel or two. A few months older than Victoria's youngest daughter, Princess Beatrice, there was a lot of gossip about their relationship and many thought they were destined to marry but he was a devout Catholic and Beatrice would need to have converted. Victoria was also keen to keep her daughter and any future husband nearby, besides she and Eugenie had high hopes for his future as Napoleon IV.

On his 18th birthday in 1874, Chislehurst celebrated him as one of their own, the railway station was decorated in his honour and flew the French tricolour whilst the waiting room was wreathed in laurels and Imperial violets with an inscription "Vive le Prince Imperial 16 mars, 1874". He must have made a great impression on the "Ladies of Chislehurst" since they gave him a very substantial present. It came from the premier Bond Street Jeweller Edwin Streeter and was a gold and silver gilt inkstand in the form of a beehive with an Imperial eagle on the lid and Napoleonic bees on the case inlaid with amethysts and his initials in diamonds and rubies.

Thousands including Frenchmen of all ranks from across the channel, artisans and earnest Bonapartists alike gathered in two enormous marquees set up in the grounds of Camden Place. One notable absentee was Prince Napoleon. An emotional mass was held for the few who could fit into the church. Queen Victoria had previously sent Napoleon's Garter standard from Windsor to be placed in the mortuary chapel where the Emperor's body was now entombed in the handsome red Aberdeen granite sarcophagus she'd given.

The Prince Imperial's speech suggested he was willing to return to France if the populace voted for such a move, reiterating the contents of a pamphlet published for French consumption a few months before which ended with the words "Everything for the People and by the People". Perhaps he hoped it would prompt some significant support for his democratic view of the future with him at the helm but there was no suggestion of any great drive to accomplish it.

18th Birthday Reception. Musée Carnavalet CCØ

The following February he passed out from Woolwich having finished 7th out of 34 and come top in fencing and riding, an excellent achievement given his English wasn't fluent. Popular amongst his fellow cadets he didn't take a commission but was allowed to join an artillery regiment based at Aldershot but wasn't earmarked for active service. His mother with an eye to his future paraded him round a few European capitals as a sovereign in waiting, meeting other Royals and the Pope. He'd been taken to the opening of Parliament, another step to learning his Imperial trade.

In May 1875 he was part of a royal style visit to the Portsmouth dockyards. The Empress was one of the many swept away by the nation's interest in a forthcoming British Artic expedition attempting to reach the North Pole. She and her ladies decided to knit some warm weather wear for the sailors on the two ships, Alert and Discovery and Eugenie presented what were called helmet caps to the crew. After her gift they were known as Eugenie Wigs or just Eugenies in naval slang. They were generally worn by the sailors to sleep in or worn under their seal skin caps when out sledging. Today we would recognise them as a form of balaclava. As a thank you the expedition named a glacier after her on the west shore of Smith Sound off Ellesmere Island, Nunavut, Canada. (She later had an archipelago in the Sea of Japan and an asteroid named after her and its moon after the Prince Imperial).

If the Prince's life was worthy, it was probably rather dull, his mother kept him on a tight financial leash, though he was seen about town but he was itching to have a more meaningful future. The problem was there was no immediate prospect of him being a real soldier. He signed up for the draft for the French army and tried to join the Austro-Hungarian forces who were involved in a war in the Balkans. They both declined to accept his services.

Then in 1879 war broke out against the Zulus in South Africa. This proved to be harder than the British expected and when his regiment were called up Louis saw it as an opportunity to prove himself. One school of thought was the young Prince was keen to separate himself from his mother's firm grip, there were even rumours of a relationship between him and a young woman which the Empress wanted to end. More importantly it gave him the opportunity to disprove the disparaging comments from some Republicans in France who portrayed him as weedy and uninspiring. Whatever the reasons both Victoria and Eugenie eventually sanctioned his request though with certain caveats and against the advice of the Prime Minister, Benjamin Disraeli. Given the rank of Lieutenant, the Prince was to be an observer, detailed to follow but not engage in any action.

He left England on the 27th February 1879 after an emotional farewell and on April 9th arrived in Durban where he joined the staff of the British commander, Lord Chelmsford as a volunteer. A few days later he marched into Zululand. Keen to see action, but too full of enthusiasm, he was warned by Lt Arthur Bigge, a close friend, "not to do anything rash and to avoid running unnecessary risks" whilst being reminded of the Empress at home and his party in France. Despite this warning Louis showed himself to be a little too impetuous when on an early mission he'd charged at some Zulus, (using the sword of his illustrious relative at the battle of Austerlitz). That alarmed the British so he was relegated to a supposedly safer role.

On June 1st he was part of a troop of eight men and a single Zulu guide that rode out on a routine reconnaissance mission to an area around Mount Itelezi just a few miles from their camp. The Prince was a talented artist and had been making sketches of the region for future missions.

At about 2.30pm, they arrived at a deserted kraal (cattle enclosure) and stopped on the banks of the Ityoyozi river to water the horses and take a break. It had been assumed they were well away from any danger so they didn't take any precautions but as they prepared to leave about 40 Zulus, some with guns ambushed the group. The Prince was an excellent horseman, but as he mounted a saddle strap broke, his foot slipped and he fell injuring his right arm as his horse bolted. Two troopers had been shot dead but the others had ridden on unaware which left the Prince to fight off the enemy attackers alone. Armed only with a revolver in his (wrong) left hand, and wounded in the leg he was overwhelmed. When a patrol found his body lying in the gulley it had been stripped naked and only a necklace was left with a medallion and a religious medal, gifts from his grandmother. The Zulus had regarded them as magical charms and being superstitious had left them untouched. There were 18 stab wounds, all on the front of his body from the native assegai, (spears), including one through his right eye.

The fateful telegram reached the Queen on the evening of June 19th and she immediately instructed Lord Sydney, the Lord of the manor, to go to Chislehurst the following morning. At 7am he messaged Eugenie's aide, the Duke of Bassano to forewarn him but before he arrived, whilst opening the post she inadvertently read a letter addressed to her secretary which mentioned the "shocking news" but didn't give any details. Alarmed by her cries, her doctor, who knew the truth said the Prince had been seriously wounded and Sydney would give her more information. Eugenie waited anxiously and rushed downstairs when he arrived but on seeing the three men standing in solemn attendance guessed the shattering news.

At first Eugenie was stunned into silence, reading and rereading the telegrams before throwing them down. A few hours later she broke down in an outpouring of grief. She spent most of the next month sitting in a darkened bedroom refusing to go outside, initially unable to eat she was sustained with a concoction of milk and rum. When the body arrived at Camden Place, she embraced the coffin, staying with it until dawn.

The recriminations began immediately questioning why he had been sent out with such a small force. It was a National embarrassment and many Bonapartists cried foul and accused the British of murder. The papers were filled with powerful tributes and Queen Victoria was one of many who paid their condolences in person, suggesting from now on the Royal widows should call each other "soeur"- sister.

The military funeral was once more held in the local church, St Mary's. The Queen visited Camden Place and placed a wreath on the coffin before it was taken to the church and then watched the procession from a platform outside. Disraeli had advised against her presence and any National show of recognition but he'd been summoned to Windsor and subjected to a 90 minute lecture on the matter. Eugenie couldn't bear to attend the service so the chief mourners who led the cortège included the Prince of Wales, and his brothers the Dukes of Edinburgh, Cambridge and Connaught. Amongst the host of other dignitaries were European royals, members of the Catholic hierarchy, Army top brass and the leading Bonapartists. His death had produced a large display of public sympathy with more than 40,000 people in the town to witness the funeral procession and pay their respects. At times the British nation surprises itself by its reactions and this was surely the case here since the 23 year old Prince was hardly a household name and was a Bonaparte, a family that had been an arch enemy but who strangely had died in the cause of British Imperialism.

There was a proposal to erect a statue in his honour at Westminster Abbey and it had some heavyweight support but Parliament voted against it, concerned it might offend the French government. Instead, the Queen had installed a substantial effigy in St George's Chapel, Windsor, and the people of Chislehurst commemorated him with a monument in the form of stone cross.

In his will, Louis nominated the son of Prince Napoleon, Prince Victor Napoleon as his successor as head of the Bonaparte party bypassing his uncle which caused a family split.

The regular army officer in the troop that tragic day, Lt Carey was court-martialled but it collapsed on a technicality though Eugenie had requested clemency and he was allowed to continue a now blighted army career.

As Eugenie contemplated her future, her grief was compounded by the death of her mother a few months later. The French government allowed her to transit the country to go to Madrid but she arrived the day before her mother died. "I am left alone, the sole remnant of a shipwreck; which proves how vain are the grandeur's of this world. I cannot even die; and God in his mercy, will give me a hundred years of my life".

Chapter Twelve

A Pilgrimage

Eugenie. LOC

From now on she wore black for the rest of her life, following Victoria's example. Eugenie then decided on two courses of action, to visit South Africa to see where her son had died and have a mausoleum built to house the bodies of her husband and son.

It was obvious that the Chislehurst church was too small and whilst it had been extended when the Emperor died, Eugenie now wanted a bespoke memorial and her elaborate plan necessitated land to build it on. Despite her best efforts the staunch Protestant owner of a large meadow which backed onto the church refused to sell and his Catholic neighbour followed suit and no other suitable options were available. The local community must have watched on anxiously since the visitors to the church were a substantial income stream. The priest Monsignor Goddard may have mixed feelings too as his church had already been was overrun after Napoleon's death. He'd even introduced entrance fees, French visitors were free on production of their identity card but others would be charged 1 shilling (5p) if they wished to pay their respects outside the normal church service hours.

Negotiations for the land purchase were still ongoing with little prospect of agreement but Eugenie was preparing for her other mission. "I feel myself drawn towards this pilgrimage as strongly as the disciples of Christ must have felt drawn towards the Holy Places. The thought of seeing, of retracing the stages of my beloved son's last journey, of seeing with my own eyes the scene upon which his dying gaze has rested, of passing the anniversary of the 1st of June watching and praying alone with his memory, is for me a spiritual necessity and an aim in life".

There must have been some worries over Eugenie's visit but Victoria generously agreed to fund the expedition and provide suitable escorts. Leading the group was Brigadier General Sir Evelyn Wood and his wife, he'd fought in the Zulu wars and had tried to dissuade Eugenie as he knew the terrain would be difficult but she was determined. Amongst the others was a widow whose husband had been killed and other soldiers who had served in the war including Arthur Bigge, who was to be the eyes and ears of the Queen. Before she left, Eugenie gave Victoria a small packet that was to be opened if she didn't return, the Queen took it with her on all her travels. When Eugenie returned she asked the Queen to open it and keep the contents which were a single cut emerald cross with diamond points known as the Andean Cross, a present on her wedding day and destined for Louis' bride, plus some strands of her hair. The Queen reciprocated with a bracelet made from her hair, a very Victorian fancy.

Eugenie embarked on The German on March 25th 1880 using her famous alias. The ship had been specially refurbished and she seemed more settled on the voyage but after arriving in Durban she was shaken to see some Zulus running in the street. The party moved on to

Pietermaritzburg for a couple of days before leaving without fuss on April 29th. It took them 26 days to reach the Tshotshosi River at the rate of 12 miles a day which Eugenie thought very slow but the cross country terrain was difficult. Her spider carriage, a type of buggy was drawn by four horses which was best suited to the dirt tracks. The group had a guard of mounted Police and totalled 75 people with around 200 horses, mules and other animals. They had to camp by the road side and set off early each morning to avoid the worst of the heat with Eugenie keen to see every place her son would have known. As they journeyed inland they realised they were being followed by a young woman. The stalker, an American calling herself Lady Avonmore was a journalist and claimed to be writing a biography of the Prince Imperial. She even tried to pass herself off as a dear friend of the Empress. Attempts to shake her off were futile and Eugenie would have nothing to do with her.

From the moment the expedition had left Pietermaritzburg, the women were dressed in white helmets, dust coats and boots, the skirts were a little shorter than usual as a precaution against snake-bite. None of Eugenie's own maids would make the trip so she borrowed one of Victoria's. Eugenie's mood was very volatile, getting worse as the trip progressed, she hardly slept and ate little. Some evenings she would walk aimlessly for miles or spend time re reading his letters. When they reached the fatal place she was extremely disappointed. She'd imagined it as a wild, romantic spot with trodden down grass but after his death almost immediately some soldiers had created a mini memorial, with a wooden cross surrounded by stones. Victoria instructed this to be upgraded to include an inscribed stone cross fixed to a concrete slab and surrounded by a wall and trees, not at all in keeping with Eugenie's vision. They did remove the concrete in an attempt to give it a more natural look and she planted some willow and ivy.

Wood took the opportunity to interview some of the Zulus involved in the ambush lured by gifts of blankets, beads and cash. They had returned his uniform and most of his belongings but Eugenie wondered why her son's watch hadn't been included, apparently the Zulus thought it was alive and had destroyed it. All those Wood spoke to insisted the Prince had fought "like a Lion", though their version was at odds with Eugenie's mental picture of events.

Prince Imperial Memorial from Queen Victoria. Wellcome Collection PD

She spent the anniversary of his death, June 1st praying by his memorial and recounted a rather mystical experience "Towards morning a strange thing happened. Although there was not a breath of air, the flames of the candles were suddenly deflected, as if someone wished to extinguish them, and I said to him: "Is it indeed you beside me'? Do you wish me to go away'?"

The party's return trip included a stop at the battlefield of Isandlwana, where some of the bones of the British dead still lay unburied from the year before. (More than 1300 British troops had been killed) Eugenie insisted they stop and spend a day burying the remains and for a couple of hours helped in the sad operation. Passing by Rorke's drift, another nearby famous clash they travelled on to Durban and set off home.

The voyage included a stop at St Helena where Napoleon Bonaparte had died in exile in 1821 and she visited every room of his dismal Longwood lodging. She also took some willow cuttings which would be planted at her new house. Her ship, The Trojan docked in Portsmouth on July 27th and she immediately returned to Chislehurst.

Chapter Thirteen

Her Hampshire Home

Having failed to make any further progress on securing the land for the mausoleum in Chislehurst, Eugenie was immediately searching for a new base and within weeks had bought Farnborough Hill in North East Hampshire.

FARNBOROUGH HILL, Residence of H.I.M. the Empress Eugenie.

Farnborough Hill c 1900.

The house, which was less than 20 years old, belonged to the widow of Thomas Longman, part of a famous publishing firm and had originally been put up for sale earlier in the year. In addition to a house, which she called a mere "cottage", there was a substantial park of 257 acres. The original auction poster described the air as salubrious and boasted of a "first class mansion in perfect order". It included "beautiful flower gardens, pleasure grounds, ornamental park and woodlands, lake and islands". There was stabling, a coach house, farm buildings and several existing workers cottages, which she would add to later and rather unusually had its own gasometer.

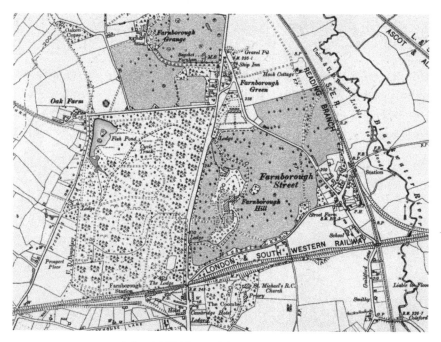

Map 1897 Hampshire Record Office

The downside was the estate was divided by a road with the woods and lake to the west and bordered on the south side by the London and South Western Railway which separated the park from the extra land bought for the Mausoleum, labelled as St. Michael's Church.

Importantly the property was near both Aldershot where the Prince had been stationed and not too far from Windsor and the Queen and easily accessible by special train or carriage. It cost £50,000 but her ambitious plans would see that amount probably treble. Whilst it sounds pretty ready made she wanted to expand the house. Her choice of architect was Hippolyte Destailleur, who'd designed Waddesdon

Manor for the Rothschild family and his brief was to add new wings, an annexe and various internal alterations to provide more rooms and space for herself, guests and staff quarters. Whilst the house retained some of the Longman Swan emblems on the brickwork, they added a symbolic **N** to the new drain pipes.

The distinguished architectural historian Sir Nikolaus Pevsner had nothing complementary to say about the end product describing it as 'an outrageously oversized chalet with an entrance tower and a lot of bargeboarding'. It was and is both unique and rather eccentric.

In January 1881 Eugenie left Camden Place, it's not clear why, perhaps Strode wanted a significant rent rise but as the building works at Farnborough would take some time she initially stayed at a cottage in Wimbledon and then another on the Queen's Osborne estate. Of course, this meant she was forced to be separated from the resting place of her husband and son. In April, on the night of the census she was staying at Windsor Castle and listed herself as ExEmpress of the French. She was extremely particular about her status and argued that whilst she was no longer Empress of the French, she would always be an Empress. That summer she spent several weeks at Chateau Arenenberg on the shore of Lake Constance in Switzerland, before occupying 28, Princes Gate, London on the edge of Hyde Park, close to the Royal Albert Hall and Buckingham Palace.

In October she was allowed to travel through France properly, on her way to Milan for the unveiling of a statue to her husband. Her return included a low key stay with friends in Paris, and a trip to Fontainebleau which had only recently been opened to tourists. This was an emotional visit, especially as she was recognised by some of the staff. When she went into the rooms used by the Prince Imperial she broke down in tears. Her misery continued when she saw the ruins of St Cloud.

Whilst she had made regular trips to Farnborough to see how the alterations were progressing, she finally moved in properly in '82, partly to expedite the building work. Construction of the Abbey and the

Imperial Crypt began in 1883 but wasn't completed until 1888. Local legend has it that Eugenie took the architect to the site and marked out the footprint with her stick. Initially the crypt was only designed for her husband and son, there was no designated resting place for Eugenie, a space was added later but changed after she died to a more prominent position created in a niche above and behind the altar. During the Abbey's construction Eugenie had kept a close eye on the progress and budget and quite probably made a few tweaks to the plans through the offices of her ever faithful secretary, Jean-Baptiste Franceschini Pietri. He'd been in the service of Napoleon since 1855, had fought and was imprisoned with him before joining the family in exile.

On completion, St Michael's Abbey (named after the patron Saint of France) was described as flamboyant French Gothic, there are elements of Gruesome Gothic too in the flying gargoyles.

St. Michael's Abbey from the Park. c1900

The Abbey was on a Hill so could be seen from the house and had a magnificent dome which dominated the skyline. She had a small pedestrian bridge built over the railway cutting so the Abbey could be reached directly from the park.

The last part of the jigsaw was a monastery which would eventually home some French Benedictine monks. She donated her wedding dress to be made into vestments along with other materials which were adapted for use by the religious order for different offices.

In 1880 Eugenie had sold her villa in Biarritz and Pietri arranged for those contents to be transported to Farnborough. There were 50 loads of furniture, paintings, tapestries and other precious goods though many arrived in poor condition and some of the paintings had been slashed deliberately by a bayonet or sharp knife.

The Hill had a staff of between 25 to 30, some were stalwarts of her Empire days and spent the rest of their lives in exile, such as Pietri, the Prince Imperial's valet Uhlmann, and Madam Lebreton, who was in charge of running the household. The Duke of Bassano was a faithful advisor and regular visitor and his son, the Marquis had escorted the Empress on her South African pilgrimage. Daughters of other Bonapartist families would come over and do a tour of duty.

Life was pretty formal, and Eugenie would be addressed as "Majeste". Her mini court had certain rules but nothing compared to life at Windsor where royal etiquette was very strict, which Eugenie found rather onerous. Desmond Mountjoy, an Irish historian, who whilst serving in London during WW1 was a regular visitor recalled how even then there remained elements of courtly deference. Going in and out of meals would be in order of precedence. Ladies staying in the house would curtsy on first seeing her in the morning and on saying goodnight, everyone else would curtsy or bow on entering and leaving her presence. At night she would be accompanied to the door of her room where she would kiss her women friends and say good night and gentlemen would kiss her hand but it was all done in a friendly, jovial manner.

For someone so used to being adorned with fabulous Jewels, she rarely wore any in exile, there was the occasional appearance of a jet clasp, or a watch on a fiddly gold chain which never kept good time, the exception were seven rings, alternating gold and silver which had belonged to former family members and were accumulated over the years.

In September 1883, Eugenie took over the cottage at Abergeldie on the Balmoral estate in Scotland for several weeks. Queen Victoria recalled a pleasant afternoon with both women working on their needlework. Victoria would distribute her creations to the poor tenants on her estates while Eugenie's work would be sent to convents "where needed". Victoria was also a keen artist and made several sketches of Eugenie which are now in the Royal collection. She was an excellent linguist and would generally write and often speak to Eugenie in French.

Balmoral is situated between Edinburgh and Inverness and the weather can be extremely changeable. Eugenie who regularly stayed on the estate was a pretty hardy soul, but Victoria seemed to positively enjoy the cold. On one visit Eugenie was invited out for a drive but after they stopped to have a cup of tea it started to snow, Victoria wasn't the least bit bothered and they stayed out despite the snowflakes falling into their drinks.

The following year the Queen made her first visit to "the Hill" so presumably the work was finished. There was one exception, a magnificent Indian carpet made by prisoners in Agra which arrived to be fitted on the gallery (hall) floor in 1886. This was similar to one made for Windsor Castle and was between 80-100ft long but the fitting didn't go according to plan as it wouldn't lie flat and they had to call in some Hindu workers from the Colonial Exhibition to manipulate it. They succeeded without touching it with their hands, everything was manoeuvred by their feet, and took nearly two hours.

The private room of the Empress had very large windows facing south as had her bedroom and dressing-room which were immediately over it. From all these rooms, for more than 30 years, she could see the mausoleum, (now mostly obscured by trees) which contained the remains of her loves and fame. Her bedroom included a porcelain bath tub, and a decorated screen. There was a glass case with some personal souvenirs including Napoleon's hat, riddled with holes from the Orsini assassination attempt. She liked to sleep with the windows open a little and her cousins revealed she wore a little fluffy night cap. Her sitting-room, or workroom, was a business like office, ridiculously overcrowded with furniture, mementoes, paintings, photographs and sculptures as were all the rooms in the house except the dining-room and the salon. She was very organised and proud to say she always paid her bills on time. Behind a bookcase was a hidden safe which held the most important documents.

She had a special room built as a precise replica of the Prince Imperial's study at Camden Place, set out exactly as it had been on the day he left for South Africa, even down to the unopened letters. An ebony cabinet included the chain and medallion the Prince had been wearing when he was killed, and nearby was his bloodied uniform. There were various childhood mementoes of the Prince and in another draw, which she never opened, was the broken saddle strap which had led to his demise.

The rescued bevelled glass and bronze doors from the Tuileries with the famous Napoleonic bees were at the end of the gallery.

Some of the Don Quixote Gobelin Tapestries from

Biarritz were hung on the side walls, with another group in the dining room. There was a conservatory with tiled window boxes in which she had planted some of the grasses and seeds she'd brought back from South Africa and which despite the contrasting temperatures had flourished. The room contained a couch, chairs and table where the Empress could work, rest or read and in pride of place was a favourite small statue of the Prince Imperial with his dog Nero.

Along the upstairs gallery were glass cases filled with autographed letters, there was even a gold tea service brought back by Bertie, the Prince of Wales from his tour of India.

The Turret chamber was the Emperor's room which included the four poster bed he'd died in and was covered with artificial memorial wreaths.

A more permanent memorial is a stone cameo relief over the fireplace in the entrance foyer.

The **N** on the drainpipes distinguished the new from old.

The Winterhalter portrait of the Empress and her Ladies from Fontainebleau was hung in the entrance hall and sold to the Louvre Museum for £3700 Guineas. (a guinea was £1 1s). There were many other significant paintings including a version of David's "Napoleon going over the Alps".

The many magnificent chandeliers and large mirrors are still in the house and the indents from her bracelets can be seen on the decorative oak staircase and balcony rail. There was a certain incongruity about how some of the objects were placed around the house, the ugly and exquisite would stand next to each other without any concern for the aesthetics and it must have felt like living in a museum.

Outside more trees were planted in the woodland, including several of her favourite fragrant pines and the willows from St Helena which, when added to the heather and rhododendrons would remind her of Compiègne.

Mountjoy thought the house a "white elephant" with little to recommend it as it was surrounded by roads and the railway line and the noise from both made walking unpleasant. Eugenie became increasingly annoyed by strangers walking in the woods ignoring the Privacy signs and one day confronted a woman, a repeat offender. I can imagine seeing the Empress dressed in black and no doubt waving her ebony stick would be enough to frighten off any trespassers. Mountjoy presumed the issues regarding space and privacy didn't bother the French as much as they did the British, "after all, the Palace of Versailles itself is on the road side"! The Empress however loved the place and always took visitors all round it to show them the views which, as she said, "were all different". She even had her own Policeman, he'd been an official fixture at Camden Place before transferring to the Hampshire force and then going into her private service.

In August 1882 Eugenie must have been thrown into emotional turmoil when the exiled Zulu King, Cetshwayo arrived in London. He'd been deposed at the end of the war in which her son had been killed by his men but many felt he'd been badly treated by the British. His cause was taken up by a newspaper and he became a celebrity during his stay. After meeting the Queen and Prime Minister the government agreed to support his attempts at restoration. It was ultimately unsuccessful and he died in '84 but Eugenie was reportedly upset by the government's stance. She left the country shortly after he arrived and spent the following two months abroad in Switzerland and Austria.

Eugenie had been involved in negotiations and litigation with the French government over the return of many of the treasures which she regarded as family property, though some of the money was basically part of their civil list (state allowance). A commission was set up to decide who got what and Eugenie was able to compile a comprehensive list from memory. Paintings and artefacts from Fontainebleau that weren't regarded as having any artistic or historic merit plus any family portraits were returned in 1881, so many Winterhalter paintings were sent to Farnborough at that time. Other court decisions went in her favour but took some time to settle, one case lasted 30 years. Less extended was the dispute in Marseilles where the city had given Napoleon some land on the coast to build a palace, the Palais de Pharo (lighthouse) and they wanted it back. In December 1882 the court found in favour of Eugenie who saw it as a victory for principle and promptly gave it back to the city. The republican council took six months before accepting the donation and it eventually became a medical school.

One treasure had found its way back shortly after they'd gone into exile, the Talisman of Charlemagne which had spent many months hidden in a kitchen cupboard. It was kept in a special shrine and the small locket style case was ornamented with precious stones and pearls. It was supposed to contain splinters of the True Cross and had been taken from the tomb of the Holy Roman Emperor Charlemagne. These relics were highly prized even if there were obvious doubts over the authenticity and had been in Napoleon's family for many decades. (It was donated by Eugenie to the Archbishop of Reims in 1919).

Whilst Eugenie was keen to have her property returned she didn't have room for everything and over time pieces were sold or donated to the French state and specific museums.

Eugenie was now a wealthy women with money and property around Europe which included a substantial inheritance from her mother's estate. She was a prudent investor and Pietri handled most of her business affairs so realistically she could do and live as she liked.

Although Eugenie's Farnborough life was pretty quiet, she always attended church in Aldershot until the Abbey was completed and supported other events in the area. Her afternoon walk often ended up at the station where she picked up the evening paper and she was a familiar and much respected figure in the area, certainly not a recluse. The keen gardeners were thrilled when she allowed the local horticultural show to be held in the grounds and presented the prizes, she even donated a silver cup for the best greenhouse plants. These shows were grand affairs with a regimental band, numerous marquees and as visitors were allowed to wander round the gardens always attracted a lot of people. Admission was 1 shilling (5p) for adults, the "labouring class" were allowed in for 3d (1.25p). Interestingly in 1887 this was held midweek, on a working day!

She maintained her links with the army and presented a cup for a regimental race and the local hare hunt continued their yearly chase in the grounds. She paid for an annual treat for around 200 children in local schools and was often on hand to witness the party. Once the house was completed these was held in the Park, and usually coincided with the Queen's birthday.

She donated solid silver cups to the local convent school though it must have been daunting for the prize winners when she came to present the awards. Not only did they have to curtsy and kiss her hand but they were then crowned with a heavy wreath of white roses and ferns held together by wire and moss, a rather unsteady coronet. Spare a thought too for the poor girl with the French prize who had to read out the thank you message, in French of course. On other occasions she would invite some of the schoolgirls up to the house for afternoon tea.

Life wasn't without entirely without incident and she narrowly avoided injury on a couple of occasions, most seriously in 1885. Returning from an afternoon ride one of the horses shied, upset by a man unloading coal and bolted and the open carriage nearly overturned. The horses ran on towards the entrance to the park and into an oncoming cart, one was killed and the passengers and coachman were thrown into the road. Fortunately, no one was seriously hurt.

Many local businesses advertised her patronage including a baker who now made French bread. Her butcher was in nearby Farnham but health standards were different then as whole uncovered carcasses were usually hung outside the shop, some just a few feet above the pavement.

Monk the Butcher in West Street, Farnham c1895

In 1886 Eugenie was joined at Farnborough by a young English woman, Agnes Carey, primarily as tutor to her cousins who were staying there. Her role was expanded to that of general companion and reference point for her English correspondence. Carey spoke excellent French, the language of "the Hill" and the Empress would tell tales of her adventures including a rather different version of her trip to Wilhelmshöhe to see the Emperor. The story now was that Eugenie had contacted Bismarck for permission to visit her husband but his curt reply warned she might get arrested if she tried. Undeterred she and Count Clary, who'd escorted the Prince Imperial back from the Franco Prussian war decided to make the visit anyway. Arriving at the castle the surprised and unsuspecting Governor presumed that such a request was officially sanctioned, and arranged rooms for their stay, whilst no doubt contacting his masters in Berlin. After a couple hours conversation with Napoleon, Eugenie retired to her room but was armed with a pass to go into town to buy a few necessities. Instead, she and the Count headed to the station, jumped on a train and headed off via a rather circuitous route home. Desperately trying not to get involved in any conversations on their journey they stopped off at The Hague. Here Eugenie wished to pay a visit to her friend, Queen Sophie of Holland but as they hadn't been able to find hotel rooms on their travels, they were a shabby looking pair. When they presented themselves at the castle they were sent on their way. Only a chance sighting by the Queen as she returned home in her carriage enabled them to gain admittance.

Farnborough Hill was a regular stopping off place for many dignitaries, numerous foreign royals and diplomats, but sometimes it was just too much as Eugenie disliked having her routine upset. Her most favourite visitor was Princess Beatrice, Victoria's youngest child who referred to Eugenie as "Aunt". Beatrice had become the Queen's chief companion and unofficial secretary and was almost permanently on call. When she was allowed to marry it was with the anticipated proviso she and her husband, Prince Henry of Battenberg had to live nearby. Eugenie became godmother to one of their daughters, Princess Victoria Eugenie, known as Ena who was born in 1887 and who married the King of Spain in 1906.

Other regulars were Sir Evelyn Wood, his wife and Dr Scott, all members of the South African party. Wood would come over on Sundays to play Tennis dressed in top hat, frock coat, linen trousers and tennis shoes and would fall to his knees on the gravel path and kiss her hand.

In 1894 the German Kaiser, William II asked to come to tea at Farnborough Hill. He was the son of Vicky, the dowager Empress, the Queen's eldest daughter who Eugenie had befriended 40 years before. The visit was brokered by Victoria who was concerned about the possible outcome, given his grandfather's role in the 1870 war. Whatever his reason it passed off without any histrionics.

She once gave a rather different tea party inviting some ladies round for a Winkle tea. Winkles are a small edible sea-snail often sold at seaside resorts. She helpfully provided her guests with gold pins to extract the delicacy from their shells and those who joined in this culinary experiment were given the pins as souvenirs!

Eugenie's daily routine was fixed, breakfast in private, then admin, reading or a short walk, lunch at 1pm was followed by an afternoon walk. The communal saying of the rosary in the private chapel led by Eugenie was at 4.45pm followed by afternoon tea in the salon at 5. Dinner was at 8pm and bed before 11pm. The silver dinner plates were part of Napoleon's campaign kit, the dessert plates were Sevres porcelain. (The grand dinner service was reserved for Royal visitors).

Carey regarded this as a typical menu (author's translation!)

Lunch October 29 1886
Turbot a l'Anglaise with capers (a favourite of the Queen)
Beef Cheeks in red wine
Roast Pheasant
Cold Ham in Jelly
Lobster in Mayonnaise
Aubergines with Cheese
Sponge cake
Desserts

That sounds very filling. Tea time was less so as Mountjoy discovered in the First World War, made worse by rationing. "A small quantity of tea was added to a small silver strainer, the hot water was then added which gave it a slight colour but to regular tea drinkers it really just tasted of hot water". The Empress drank the first cup with a little milk and Mountjoy felt glad her eyesight was failing so "she couldn't see the revolting black tea dust floating on top" She gave her sugar ration to him as he was a soldier and the rest of the feast was a piece of bread or toast with a little bit of jam, scraped off a plate with gilt spoons. Once everyone had received their first cup of tea the Empress would have her second which would be colder and even worse than the first.

Even in her dotage her temper could still flare up. Any dinner table comments she disagreed with could be marked by some animated gesturing, rapier like with the toothpick, often with a fierce stare that could freeze the blood of any opponent. She wasn't averse to a bout of glass thumping on the table either but any harsh words would be smoothed over later.

Although Eugenie steadfastly refused to be a celebrity she was inundated with mail, most of it begging letters or requests for patronage. She had a strict system to deal with her correspondence. She opened all the letters herself and put them into three piles, "Accept, Refuse and Investigate" and divided those that needed attention between Pietri and Madame Lebreton. Every so often she would personally burn unwanted documents as she was determined to maintain her privacy. In the days before she'd fled the Tuileries she'd destroyed any incriminating papers by tearing them into pieces and pulping them with water in a bath, having already sent many important documents out of the country.

In the mid 1880's preparations were underway for a Napoleonic museum near the coach house in the park. There were already two lavish Imperial state coaches on site, one of which was used for her wedding, lined with satin, another was Napoleon's favourite carriage which he would drive round the city. When completed it included some notable and remarkable pieces of Bonaparte history, Napoleon I's signature grey overcoat and cocked hat, sticks, swords and uniforms, his coronation robes and those of Josephine, plus numerous pieces of Louis XVI furniture and possessions. Her husband and son were well represented including the Emperor's death mask which was usually kept covered. There was a 10-12foot replica of the iconic Bonaparte memorial, the Vendome column in Paris. This had been pulled down by the Communards which resulted in crowds rushing to gather souvenirs, reminiscent of what happened when the Berlin Wall came down. The most obvious omission from the extensive collection was that nothing of her own was included.

In September 1887, a red granite sarcophagus for the Prince Imperial, ordered by the Empress, arrived from Aberdeen and at the same time Napoleon's identical one was brought from Chislehurst to St Michael's Abbey. A few months later on January 9th, the 15th anniversary of Napoleon's death, the coffins of the Emperor and the Prince Imperial were transferred from Chislehurst to the Mausoleum with military formalities. Princess Beatrice sent a permanent memorial wreath of white porcelain flowers which is adjacent to the Prince's tomb.

The crypt was set out with Napoleon on one side of the central altar and his son on the other. Local stories say the French objected to Napoleon being buried on English soil so a layer of neutral Swiss soil was imported to create a diplomatic separation.

Every so often there are calls, sometimes by French government officials, for the remains of Napoleon to be sent back to France (as had been done decades before with the body of King Louis Philippe who'd been buried in Weybridge). They have been rebuffed quite forcibly and that attitude is unlikely to change.

Chapter Fourteen

The Traveller

From 1890 onwards Eugenie embarked on a series of travels that belied her age. The newspapers regularly tracked her progress, though not always accurately, sometimes it was just a short reference to her arriving or leaving a country or more simply, "the Empress passed through Paris unmolested".

In July that year she went north on a 3 week cruise to the Norwegian Fjords, her cabin having been specially furnished with Liberty curtains. A short visit to Osborne followed and in September it was reported she'd gone to watch the famous passion play at Oberammergau in the company of the exiled Queen of Spain, Isabella II. Eugenie had been one of her bridesmaids and ironically the Queen was now exiled in France. The passion play is held in a small German village in Bavaria and has been performed since 1634, normally every 10 years. By tradition this is staged on open air platforms, with only the privileged few sitting undercover. The spectacle that year ran for nearly eight hours, starting at 8am and finishing at 5pm with just one break for lunch. Their visit was marred by extremely cold weather so they left early, only to be kept waiting for two hours on the station platform at Murnau.

One element of British life that didn't agree with Eugenie was the cold damp winters which she blamed for her Rheumatism and Bronchitis. Despite encouragement from some to move from her "dull little village" to somewhere with a better climate, she decided instead to seek treatment for her Rheumatism in Amsterdam. A world famous clinic there was run by Dr Johann Metzger who relied on massage to work his cures and was inundated with patients, all of whom he charged a flat fee, regardless of status. He refused to make house calls, those arriving at his clinic were seen on a first come first serve system, each patient waiting in a cubicle until it was their turn. His progress through the daily list was punctuated by the screams of the sufferers as he worked his magic, rather roughly with his "golden thumbs". Eugenie became very nervous and tense whilst waiting which made the treatment more difficult. She was on the verge of giving up when they persuaded the Doctor to treat her first each session which alleviated her anxiety. Metzger is regarded as one of the fathers of physiotherapy and the inventor the Swedish Massage.

Whilst the treatment might have helped, she began to think about an alternative. During her time at Camden Place she would normally retreat to Florence but despite having central heating put into Farnborough Hill what she really wanted was a proper winter home.

In the late 1880's a British consortium bought a large tract of land around Cap Martin in the south of France and developed a private estate. Located between the fashionable resort of Menton and Monte Carlo, the French Riviera was popular with European aristocracy and the wealthy sun seekers. It was also a favourite of Queen Victoria who would travel there under the alias of the Duchess of Balmoral.

The first project was the luxury Grand Hotel designed by Danish architect Hans Georg Tersling and it was an immediate success. Amongst those early guests was Eugenie and she commissioned him to build a villa but had to wait for French government permission before construction could start as they were wary of allowing her a permanent base in the country. Tersling had worked in Monte Carlo with Charles Garnier who Eugenie knew from her Empire days. Called Cyrnos, meaning Corsica in Greek this was a nod to Napoleon I's birthplace.

Villa Cyrnos ©old books image/Alamy Photo Stock

The furniture arrived from Farnborough in early 1894 and from 1895 onwards, except during the war, she would spend part of every year in residence.

Transforming the land was a major enterprise as her two hectare estate was wooded, scrubby land with barren soil pitted with large rocks, but undeterred she commissioned a grand garden. For two years, 28 workers transformed it into what contemporaries regarded as the most beautiful garden on the Côte d'Azur. The genius behind the creation was a German landscape designer, Ludwig Winter. He'd once been employed as a gardner at the Tuileries but was sacked for singing the Marseillaise, the Republican anthem in the presence of the Empress. The Empire used "Partant pour le Syrie", a ballad handily composed by the Emperor's mother, Queen Hortense.

The first job was to blast away at the rock with dynamite before importing good quality soil by the cart load from nearby hills. The centre pieces were a couple of giant palm trees, 11 metres high and weighing around 16 tonnes which required 18 horses to transport them from Winter's personal nursery. Once on site it took a combination of 30 men and some heavyweight machinery to position them upright.

Eugenie as you probably guessed didn't want a traditional English country garden of manicured lawns and neat flowerbeds. The result was a mixture of the wild, wonderful and fragrant. Wisteria, the symbolic violets, roses, orange trees, jasmine, magnolia and many more exotic and native species were spread throughout. There was even a vegetable garden, six beehives and for good measure, a couple of goats. One modern perfume manufacturer produced a scent which sought to replicate the fragrant garden, presumably minus the goats.

The large white faced Italian style villa, came with a marble staircase, impressive colonnades, balconies and several guest rooms. Her own bedroom looked out over the Mediterranean towards Monte Carlo and Eugenie loved to spend time relaxing on the terrace. Like Farnborough Hill it was "very Empire" and incorporated another mini Napoleonic museum plus Louis XVI furniture, Sèvres porcelain and numerous important paintings. Its splendid gardens attracted many notable visitors. Queen Victoria, complete with her donkey cart would pop over for tea when in residence nearby. Empress Sisi of Austria, a frequent guest, had a key to the garden gate from the coastal path to use on her extended morning walks. Sisi spent her later years estranged from her family wandering round Europe and was assassinated in Geneva in 1898 by an Italian anarchist. Rather bizarrely her husband, the Emperor Franz Joseph then sent Eugenie the parasol and fan she'd had with her when she was killed.

Numerous heads of state made a beeline for Cyrnos and others included the novelist Jean Cocteau, sculptor Auguste Rodin and designer Coco Chanel, so a pretty eclectic bunch of guests. Cyrnos was so popular that she had an additional but much smaller property built nearby to cope with the overflow, the Villa Teba, the name reflecting her Spanish title.

She invited many young relatives and even encouraged them to bring a friend. Her great, great niece Vittoria Colonna, Duchess of Sermoneta was a regular at both Farnborough and Cyrnos. On one occasion she arrived at the villa minus her luggage which had got lost. She desperately wanted to go to the casino in Monte Carlo but reluctantly decided her travelling clothes weren't suitable, the Empress thought all that was required was the addition of a hat. She had three all with a specific name, Trottinette (for walks), the Va-t-en-ville (shopping) and Le Glorieux (the Glorious) which was reserved for special occasions. This, Eugenie thought was just the one for the casino as it was distinguished by three large plumes and would certainly have made an impression. The young Duchess perhaps understandingly declined though she did take up the opportunity to try on a couple of Eugenie's old Empire dresses. Her view on the crinoline "charming and made one feel like an animated flower but the quaint little bodices were quite impossible to squeeze into".

Eugenie appears to have had quite an affinity with young people and although she never went to the casino herself would often send these visitors off in her car sometimes with a 'Louis' (fr20 coin) to put on the roulette wheel. It never won.

In 2021 the ruler of Monaco, HSH Prince Albert II unveiled a marble bust of Eugenie to commemorate her relationship with the Principality. It also marked the anniversary of her death (1920) and that of Prince Albert I (1922) who was a great friend. The bust is a copy of one at Compiègne and is in the gardens of Fort Antoine in Monte Carlo positioned so she gazes in the direction of her villa.

Eugenie would normally come to Cyrnos by train stopping off in Paris where she would take a suite at the Hotel Continental which overlooked the Tuileries gardens and which must have evoked many memories. Its address is Rue de Castiglione, a name which had its own significance. She even met up with her nemesis Princess Mathilde which suggests they were on better terms.

Not all her travels were abroad, on a trip to Bournemouth she visited the Royal Bath Hotel where she was surprised to find a favourite Louis XVI cabinet on display. She sent the owner, Merton Russell-Cotes a diamond, no doubt hoping for the cabinet in exchange but he was a canny operator and kept both the cabinet and the diamond. His house became the Russell-Cotes Museum where the cabinet is now on show.

The Imperial name is now associated with a traditional event in the town. For health reasons a doctor recommended early evening walks through the Lower Gardens down to the beach. The Empress came up with the idea to light the path with floating candles in coloured glass. The only problem is which Empress, most attribute the idea to Eugenie but others to Empress Sisi but the festival of candles is still a regular celebration.

Eugenie was always keen on new inventions and in September 1896 she saw one of the first proper film shows. Lantern slide entertainments had been around for some years but early projectors started to appear and C. Goodwin Norton, one of the pioneers, began producing and showing films. She was at the home of Lord and Lady Pirbright at nearby Henley Park and was keen to have the process explained to her which Lord Pirbright, who'd mastered the details obligingly did so in French.

Queen Victoria was treated to one of Godwin's shows 6 months later and early cinemas, or electric theatres began to appear from this period. Eugenie became quite a fan of Charlie Chaplin but had she lived a few years longer she could have seen herself immortalised in an early silent French movie called Imperial Violets screened in 1923. It was remade in 1936 and as a musical in 1952. The plot is about a young gypsy woman who foretells Eugenie will become Empress and then saves her from an attempt on her life. The character of Eugenie has appeared in several other films over the years.

According to her companions, the one Imperial trapping she really missed was the Yacht, L'Aigle, so it was perhaps no surprise that in 1896 the Empress bought a boat. The Thistle was a very impressive three masted steam yacht which had been owned by the 12th Duke of Hamilton, the son of the friends she had known from her Empire days. He was seldom seen on his Scottish estates and was based instead in Suffolk to facilitate his interests in gambling, horse racing and sailing. Vanity Fair pulled no punches in 1873 when assessing his character "it is the curse of his life that he has never learnt to find pleasure in aught but idleness". He weighed in at 20 stone and suffered from a variety of illnesses and died aged 50 in 1895 whilst staying on the yacht in Algiers. He'd run up enormous debts so when the boat came up for sale the following year, she bought it.

The Thistle had been launched in 1881 and was a luxurious 190ft long vessel with 6 master cabins and capable of around 12 knots. It needed a crew of 23 plus her cooks, butlers and footmen when she was on board.

The yacht sounds ideal but it wasn't very stable in rough conditions and only those impervious to seasickness, like Eugenie, would readily accept an invitation to sail in her if there was any prospect of rough water. One guest, Ethel Smyth, was onboard on a stormy outing round the Mull of Kintyre, off south west Scotland, whilst most hid away Eugenie insisted on having a chair strapped to a mast so she could experience the storm.

She added a few mod cons to the yacht including an early gramophone (device for playing music) and wireless telegraphy system. Eugenie would regularly sail up and down the Mediterranean and was ever present at the Regatta weeks at Cowes on the Isle of Wight. This was the yachting capital of the country and acted like a summer camp for European Royals. At some stage she met a fellow sailing enthusiast Sir Thomas Lipton who was to be a long term friend. His background couldn't have been more different. Born in the Glasgow slums of poor Irish immigrant parents he tried his luck in the US when just 15, sailing across the Atlantic with hope but little money. He worked on rice and tobacco plantations, made good use of his Celtic background when mixing with fellow emigres but it was as an assistant in a grocery store in New York that he learnt a few tricks that would help make his fortune. When he returned home he revamped his parent's little grocery shop and 10 years later had more than 300 stores across the country.

Sir Thomas Lipton.
1848-1931 LOC

Lipton's marketing campaigns were years ahead of his competitors and the self-publicist in him was reflected in the 80 plus folios he kept of his press cuttings.

He expanded his empire to include tea plantations in Ceylon (Sri Lanka). Tea had gained popularity across the social spectrum in Britain during the latter decades of the century through a combination of tax cuts and Lipton's trading methods which undercut his competitors and helped make it more affordable.

His passion was yachting despite knowing little of how to sail a boat himself, and he pumped thousands into his hobby. It connected him to an elite social circle of Kings and Princes but he was blackballed (rejected) by the Royal Yacht Squadron for many years, basically because he was a grocer and therefore not a gentleman. Ironically the Grocer's Federation didn't want him either because of his commercial tactics. (The membership committees in many institutions would vote in secret by the use of two balls, white to accept, black to oppose).

Lipton set his sights on winning the America's Cup, the prestigious competition between a chosen yacht of Britain and the US. He tried five times with his famous competition boats all called Shamrock and lost on each occasion but was rewarded with a cup as the best loser. His campaigns brought him public fame in the US and enabled him to make another fortune there. He was knighted in 1901 by his fellow sailing enthusiast King Edward VII.

Lipton was a regular visitor to Cap Martin and Eugenie a frequent passenger on his luxury yacht, the Erin. (During the First World War both their vessels were handed over to the Royal Navy. The Thistle's service was short lived, five months from October 1914 as her instability nearly resulted in a sinking in rough water in the North Sea. The yacht was decommissioned and sold shortly afterwards. The Erin renamed the Aegusa was sunk by mines whilst on patrol in the Mediterranean in 1916 off Malta whilst trying to pick up survivors from another ship).

In July 1903 Eugenie was in Venice, and Lady Layard came on board, initially to sign the visitor's book. She found her knitting, though well wrapped up as it was unseasonably cold but thought her "sadly changed" having lost "every good look and all her smartness". Her eyebrows were one long painted black streak on each side with her signature black lines under her eyelids, though she'd forgotten to do one side! Well, we all have bad days.

In 1905 Eugenie paid a return visit to Egypt, it was 36 years since she'd visited the country to open the Suez Canal and much had changed. The Canal hadn't been fully finished when it opened and took a few years to reach its full potential. The Egyptians were left with a huge debt partly due to the Khedive's attempt to transform Cairo into a western style city with a massive building programme. The British Government had initially viewed the Canal project with suspicion and chosen not to invest but now appreciated the great benefit it brought to their trade, cutting several days off the journey time to India and soon most of the shipping through the Canal was British.

In 1875, the Egyptian government needing money to pay off their spiralling debts offered their 44% share of the Canal company for sale. The British Prime Minister, Benjamin Disraeli jumped at the chance but didn't go through normal parliamentary channels, instead, in a matter of hours he arranged to borrow the required £4 million from Rothschild's bank, (around £250 million in 2022.) The head of the bank was a personal friend and the deal was done so quickly there was no formal documentation and was completed on the basis of a gentleman's agreement between the two men. The purchase was well received and the loan paid off within 5 months.

The British involvement intensified in 1882 when Egypt became what was known as the "veiled protectorate" with British troops in residence. Thomas Cook, the premier travel agents were now the most influential company in the country providing many locals with their livelihood. They set up a major hub at Port Said at the northern mouth of the Canal servicing more than two dozen vessels taking tourists up and down the Nile on their popular holiday trips. Their cruise liners which doubled as mail ships used the waterway on their journeys to

Ceylon, Madras (Chennai), Hong Kong, Singapore and beyond, linking the major Empire ports. Had you been a passenger going ashore in Port Said you would have found quayside vendors happy to accept British pounds and if you took a donkey ride into town you might have been amused to discover they'd all been given British names, Gladstone and Disraeli would bray at each other, much like they did in Parliament and Lily Langtry was on hand to brighten up your day maybe on your way to the casino.

In 1905 Egypt was the place to be and the social scene in January that year was marked by a large contingent of European aristocracy mixed with wealthy tourists including many Americans and in their midst was Eugenie. She'd sailed from Marseilles on the Macedonia and like many appreciated that Egypt offered a near perfect climate at that time of year. The seemingly perpetual sunshine and dry conditions had weaned the social elite away from their normal Mediterranean haunts. The entertainment that season was on a par with Nice or Monte Carlo with balls and fetes and the best hotels were turning away guests. Amongst the winter visitors were her neighbours at Bagshot Park, the Duke and Duchess of Connaught and their family. During their stay their daughter Princess Margaret met and became engaged to the future King of Sweden, Gustav VI Adolf.

The Palace where she had stayed for the Inauguration of Suez had become a hotel, and retains some features and portraits reflecting the Second Empire. Like many she travelled to the Valley of the Kings at Luxor to see the excavations of the Theban Tombs. In February that year the archaeological teams discovered the Royal tomb of Yuya and Tuya, the most important Royal burial find until Tutankhamen. Although it had been looted during the previous centuries many treasures still remained including magnificent funerary furniture, jewellery, scarabs, seals, crockery, musical instruments and statues. After three weeks most of the artefacts had been packed up but there was one chair remaining, one of the star finds. It was gilded carved wood with panelled scenes and a woven reed seat and belonged to the ancient Egyptian Princess Sitamun.

Throne of Princess Sitamun. CCØ

Just as they were about to finish their work Eugenie arrived, insisting she wanted to go down into the tomb.

The archaeologists could hear a man addressing her in French as "Your highness," begging her not to tire herself out. A few minutes later she appeared inside the tomb, wearing a dirty old coat and a funny cloche hat and walking with a cane. The supervising archaeologist James Quibbell apologised saying they were practically finished and he had no chairs available "Why there" she said "that there will do me nicely" and sat down in the 3,000 year old Throne of Princess Sitamun. Thankfully it was sturdy enough not to give way. She then remarked on the Empire style of the curved heads on the chair and suddenly they recognised her but were too polite to ask her to stand up.

Leaving Luxor, she sailed up river on a dahabeyah, a small houseboat, to Aswan, a popular luxury health resort.

On May 5th 1906 Eugenie celebrated her 80th birthday at her French villa, although she'd long since stopped marking her anniversaries she was thrilled to receive a congratulatory message from the Emperor Franz Joseph. Later that month she surprisingly opted not to attend the wedding of her god daughter, Princess Victoria Eugenie (Ena) to the King of Spain. The wedding day turned out to be traumatic as a bomb was thrown at their carriage as they drove from the church, it missed them but several people were killed, hundreds injured and Ena's dress was spattered with blood. Eugenie's wedding present was a fan, at first sight rather underwhelming, it wasn't until much later that Ena opened the box properly and nine fabulous square cut emeralds fell out. They'd been part of the Imperial Fontenay tiara and maybe her fairy godmother was trying to avoid customs duties.

A few weeks after her birthday Eugenie achieved another milestone as she "climbed" Vesuvius. I'm not convinced she actually climbed it as her trip coincided with the aftermath of a major eruption of Mount Vesuvius. This killed several hundred, injured many more with thousands made homeless, some by lava but more by the ash that was scattered across the region. Given the circumstances it would be a surprise to find her anywhere near the Volcano but although the eruption, which began on the 7th April did considerable damage it wasn't totally off limits.

In the 1880's the crater was accessible via a funicular and the popular song "Funiculi, Funicular" was written to commemorate the achievement. In 1904 Thomas Cook opened a more efficient single track railway and along with other improvements meant it could cope with the thousands of tourists who wanted to go to the top. They built a hotel called the Hermitage half way up the hillside at Eremo claiming the air there "was transparent and pure". Whilst part of the funicular was destroyed in the eruption the rail line was dug out of the ash and back in service 12 days later. The line passed by the Observatory positioned on the slopes at Eremo to monitor volcanic activity in the region and which had stayed open and manned throughout. Eugenie arrived in late May, lunched at the Hotel and then toured the Observatory with Professor Matteucci.

Eugenie on the steps of the Observatory.
The Graphic 1906 © Mary Evans Picture Library

It's doubtful she "climbed" up further but she did travel on to Pompeii, scene of the famous eruption of AD 79.

Her next stop was Venice but her return to Farnborough was disrupted by an outbreak of Typhus on the Thistle so she went by train to Ischl, the summer residence of Franz Joseph, prompted by his birthday message. She had a soft spot for the Austrian Emperor and was thrilled that he addressed her as "Your Majesty" and wore the ribbon of the Legion d'honneur given him by Napoleon.

That same year she donated the Swiss Chateau of Arenenberg to the canton of Thurgau and sent some of its Napoleonic mementoes to the Chateau Malmaison in Paris which had recently opened as a museum.

Eugenie was an inveterate traveller and in August 1907 she swopped the Med for the chillier waters of the Baltic. Having moored in Bergen in Norway she was surprised to see the yacht and "battleship" escort of German Kaiser William ll arrive in the harbour. He immediately sent an equerry to see if he could visit. With her was Isabel Vesey, a regular companion in later years having been recruited originally to be the 14th person at a dinner party. She didn't think him imposing but noted his piercing eyes and felt he would have been more comfortable in uniform. Instead, he arrived at 11am in a blue serge suit with "too many rings, a bracelet and bright yellow shoes". The visit lasted more than 90 minutes but Eugenie was determined not to invite him to lunch! It made a sensational headline in a French magazine but was regarded as a courteous meeting. He was however annoyed that Eugenie had some memorabilia of her friendship with Victoria, whilst he, her grandson, who had been at her bedside when she died had received nothing. On learning Eugenie was leaving the following morning he ordered his escort ships to fly the French flag and fire a gun salute as the Thistle departed, but it was at 7am and Eugenie slept through it.

Much more congenial was the private visit of the King and Queen of Spain (her goddaughter) to Farnborough Hill in November 1907. It came as a surprise to the townsfolk but as darkness fell the drive to the house was illuminated with a series of red lamps hung from poles. Canopies and decorations were added to the exterior of the house and flowers filled the main rooms as a steady stream of dignitaries arrived for dinner. The men were in court dress or uniform and the ladies in their best frocks and all except Eugenie wore their jewels. The table was lit by candles from silver candlesticks and the bandsmen of the 16th Lancers played during the meal. After dinner there was a reception with some of the leading local families invited to join the party. All this was followed at 10pm by an entertainment featuring the band of the Coldstream guards plus songs, a sketch from one of the most famous comedians of the period Harry Tate and a few magic tricks from another notable performer Nate Leipzig. To cap it off a buffet supper was then served. It sounds like an extraordinary evening, far removed from normal life at the Hill and I imagine the lucky locals would have dined out on their invitation for months. Whilst it wasn't Versailles perhaps it brought back some happy memories of her Empire days.

Around the same time she was planning her next adventure calling on the experience of Thomas Lipton, though the message from her secretary rather surprised him. "The Empress would like you to arrange for her to go to Ceylon. You praised the beauties of the island so enthusiastically to Her Majesty when you were last here that nothing will dissuade her from going. She has set her heart on the trip and wants you, as a favour, to make all arrangements as soon as you can". She was 81 at the time which must have been a concern to Lipton, however he made the necessary preparations and set off in advance to ensure everything was ready for her arrival.

Eugenie embarked at Marseilles on the P and O liner RMS Mooltan on January 10th 1908. Although she used her famous alias it's unlikely anyone on board was fooled since the crew routinely addressed her as "Your Majesty" and word soon got round. A special cabin had been arranged, knocking two into one and with her entourage, including a medical attendant, she appeared throughout as stately but understated. Fellow passengers reported that she appeared on deck around 11ish and stayed around until late in the evening, frequently spending time reading in the music room if the weather turned chilly.

Lipton was waiting to greet her and she was cheered by locals on her arrival as she was the first important person to have visited the island.

Her initial stay in Colombo was in special apartments in the now opulent Galle face hotel. The current hotel now has the obligatory Empress suite, it consists of three rooms and three balconies overlooking the ocean. She then travelled inland to Kandy to see the famous Temple of the (Buddha's) Tooth. Leonard Woolf, a government agent in the district met her and was invited to tea, she possibly thought he was more important than he was. He wasn't overly enamoured describing this once renowned beauty as "positively ugly" a tiny, white haired, little bent old woman, dressed in black. Nor was he impressed by her demeanour, although affable he thought she expected the same etiquette and ceremony due to the wife of a reigning monarch.

Hugh Clifford, the Governor General of Ceylon accompanied her to the opening of the inner sanctum of the Buddhist shrine, a rare event. Eugenie spent seven weeks on the island and described it as "One of the most delightful holidays that she had ever spent", much to the relief of Lipton as he was well known for his embellished story telling.

Eugenie had intended on travelling on to India, no doubt fuelled by tales from Bertie, who as Prince of Wales had represented Victoria on a Royal visit there in 1875/6. At some stage illness intervened and she re-joined the Mooltan for the return leg.

In 1909 she was in Madrid in May and Ireland in July which included shooting the rapids in the lakes at Killarney. She once more demonstrated her great capacity to absorb information, show interest and say the right things, an invaluable skill during her Imperial days.

In 1910 Vesey joined her summer adventures as they sailed a total of 3758 miles in 3 months across the Med including a long awaited return to Constantinople. The old Sultan had died but Eugenie was afforded a regal welcome and loaned a small launch to travel down the coast. It was a little too ostentatious for their needs as they sat on deck in gold brocaded chairs but Eugenie loved to go onshore and mingle with the locals as she was fascinated by the East and the local customs.

Her trips to France were now a regular part of her year and in 1910 she revisited Compiègne, discreetly joining a guided tour. What memories must have been stirred and when the tour reached the Prince Imperial's bedroom she nearly fainted and asked for a chair and a glass of water. As she raised her veil the guide recognised her and as the others moved on Eugenie was allowed to stay in the room by herself for ten minutes.

In between all these adventures she returned to Farnborough Hill. In 1883, she had met a new neighbour (Dame) Ethel Smyth, a notable composer. She was fluent in French and would initially ride over from nearby Frimley on her bicycle and then change into evening wear in the bushes, once the Empress heard about this ruse she insisted on sending a carriage. Although Eugenie had been in England for more than a decade her English still had a few peculiarities, most noticeably that she dropped her 'h's and Smyth witnessed some entertaining conversations. One day the Empress joined her ride home but the coachman was a little erratic and not always that sober and on this occasion one of the rear wheels clipped the gatepost of Smyth's house, "pulling up, he explained that the 'orses were pulling very 'ard. The Empress's angry rejoinder was: It's not the 'orses that are pulling 'ard, it's you that always forget the be'ind of the carriage".

Although Eugenie wasn't musical, in fact "totally devoid of musical instinct" according to Smyth she was keen to promote her work and paid for the printing of some of her early compositions, in particular a large scale choral work, the Mass in D. In 1891 Smyth was taken to Cap Martin and a few months later when she'd finished the score accompanied Eugenie to Scotland where she was invited by the Queen to Balmoral and gave a solo rendition of the work, accompanying herself on the piano. The result was the Duke of Edinburgh, Prince Alfred asked the Royal Choral Society to perform the Mass, which they did in January 1893 at the Royal Albert Hall. It was the only official public appearance Eugenie made after the Prince Imperial died.

In 1910 Smyth became a suffragist, wrote their anthem "The March of the Women" and was jailed for throwing a stone through the window of a government minister. Whilst in Holloway prison she was seen by one of her visitors, the conductor, Sir Thomas Beecham, hanging out of her cell window directing her fellow inmates with a toothbrush as they sang the song whilst marching round the exercise yard. She would later entertain guests at the Hill with tales of her exploits.

138

Eugenie had established her feminist credentials fifty years before so presumably supported the cause but probably not their methods but she was delighted when Smyth introduced her to the suffragette leader, Emmeline Pankhurst who became a frequent lunch guest.

Another composer and neighbour Sir Arthur Sullivan no doubt surprised her with tales of his grandfather who was paymaster on St. Helena when Bonaparte was in exile. When the prisoner died in 1821 his heart was taken out supposedly to be sent to his wife, Marie Louise. Kept overnight in a basin Thomas Sullivan's version was he stood guard with his gun to shoot any rats that came near. The island was overrun with them but there were many alternative tales about what happened to the heart. One of the doctors present at the autopsy reported that a rat did get hold of it and was dragging it across the floor when it was rescued. Another scurrilous version suggested the rats succeeded and a sheep's heart was substituted, his wife certainly didn't receive the gruesome gift but short of a DNA test lets presume the original was buried with the body in St Helena. The French government didn't want Bonaparte's remains in Paris at that time but his coffin was eventually returned to France 19 years later and he is now entombed in Les Invalides.

In general Eugenie stayed clear of French politics but there were notable exceptions. When Prince Napoleon was arrested in January 1883 after issuing a manifesto suggesting he was the best man to run the country she rashly rushed over to Paris to see if she could help. She didn't stay long and Victoria thought her very courageous.

In December 1894, a Jewish Army officer called Alfred Dreyfus was convicted of treason for spying for the Germans. He was sentenced to life imprisonment in the infamous Devil's Island prison in French Guinea (South America). New evidence was eventually produced which proved his innocence but it wasn't quite that simple as the army tried to cover it up even after the real culprit had been exposed.

The whole affair lasted for 12 years and divided the country amidst a wave of anti-Semitic demonstrations. The Empress publicly supported Dreyfus which resulted in a personal attack by a French magazine. It's amazing how she was still hated in some quarters and opponents continued to take pot shots at her as they had done for more than 30 years.

Chapter Fifteen

The Final Years

Drawing by Ferdinand Bac 1912 at Villa
Cyrnos. Palais Fesch Musée des beaux-arts

© RMN -Grand Palais / cliché Stéphane Maréchalle

The turn of the century brought the death of Queen Victoria in 1901 which was a great blow, "it is for me a terrible grief to lose a sincere and affectionate friend with whom I could speak freely".

Many other old friends and foes passed away in this period, Prince Napoleon in 1891, Madame Lebreton in 1899, and Princess Mathilde in

1904. Victoria's two children, who'd she first met in 1855 also died, Vicky in '01 and her brother King Edward VII in 1910. A few years later she suffered another major loss, her loyal secretary, Pietri died in 1915. He is buried next to the door to the crypt, and his nephew took on the role of secretary.

Eugenie had always been an avid reader, but much preferred history or science to frothy novels. She was keen to buy new gadgets and Farnborough Hill had both a telephone and electric lighting well ahead of her neighbours. When Guglielmo Marconi was experimenting with his wireless telegraphy system she lent him her yacht to help with his early work at sea. Transatlantic communications were initiated in December 1901 between Cornwall and Canada, the first proper message went to the King, Eugenie received the second.

She had a fascination for air travel of all sorts, she'd met a famous balloonist, Santos Dumont in Cap Martin in 1902 and Farnborough had developed into an important aeronautical centre, initially with balloons and then aeroplanes.

In 1909, one of the pioneer pilots Samuel Cody who'd completed the first flight in Britain was demonstrating his new bi-plane to a fascinated crowd above his Farnborough base. After the flight he was introduced to the Empress who impressed him by her grasp of the technicalities. She always wanted to fly but never got the chance.

Having had a few problems with horse drawn transport she bought a car, a large black and green

Renault, but her chauffeur was rather erratic and Eugenie disliked speeding. Once the vehicle and its passengers had to be rescued from a ditch by a steam roller and in 1913 he was fined £5 for speeding after a nasty collision with a cyclist who was left with several broken bones.

When the Archduke Franz Ferdinand, the heir to the Austrian throne was assassinated on June 28th 1914 Eugenie returned home from her travels, she knew enough about the state of play in Europe to know that meant trouble. She returned via Paris and visited the gardens of the Tuileries only to be told off for picking a flower and then bade a private farewell to Fontainebleau. When war was declared in August, she quickly offered a wing of her house as a hospital and convalescent home for officers. It had eight rooms, a communal lounge, smoking room and an operating theatre which had been converted from a bathroom. She paid for everything and ensured the hospital was equipped with the most modern equipment. There were novel outdoor cubicles in the park which had room for a bed and a chair for visitors so patients could take advantage of any good weather and of course the fresh air. For others there was tennis, croquet and chess.

To avoid upsetting the French the patients were Belgian and British and the hospital was run by Lady Dorothy Haig, wife of one of the British Generals. Her regime was efficient, innovative but quite autocratic and Eugenie felt rather excluded. When Haig resigned in 1915, Vesey, the daughter of a Major General took charge and the new regime was more accommodating. Eugenie would make daily tours, always keen to try out any new equipment and there was the occasional morale boosting Royal visit.

One young officer, Lt Philip Bateman, wounded on the western front in 1915 was sent to the hospital. "The atmosphere was delightful and patients were at once made to feel that they were honoured guests at a country-house party".

Eugenie was herself treated in the hospital after falling down the house stairs which must have been of great concern given her age, fortunately she wasn't badly hurt.

She was passionately supportive of England and confident of Allied success and had hoped to send a fleet of ambulances to France and set up a field hospital at Cyrnos but their government refused the offers, instead she supported many French hospitals and their Red Cross with substantial donations but requested no acknowledgement.

The Bonaparte heir, Prince Victor Napoleon, his wife Princess Clementine and family who'd had to escape from Belgium came to live in the Hill. Their two young children were probably the only light relief for her in this dismal period. Amongst her visitors was the Empress Maria Feodorovna, mother of Tsar Nicholas II, she'd escaped Russia before the murder of her son and his family and was on her way to exile in her native Denmark. She was accompanied by her sister the Dowager Queen Alexandra, the widow of Bertie, King Edward VII.

Mountjoy, when his duties at the War office allowed brought a diverse series of guests from around the world to meet and entertain her which gave Eugenie the opportunity to do some polite interrogation on the world as they saw it.

Her eyesight had deteriorated significantly but it was good enough to watch from the terrace any airborne Zeppelin action heading in their direction. She relished being near a potential war zone, others were less keen and of course the dome of St Michael's was an excellent landmark for pilots returning to their Farnborough base or enemy attackers. She followed the news avidly with great insight, helped by regular phone calls from the King and most likely saw

German prisoners of war from their nearby camp who were involved in work parties in the town.

Many of her staff had been called up as were several monks by their native armies. Two Brothers won the Croix de Guerre and Dom Godu had his presented at the Abbey after the war by the French Army's chief of staff and future head of government, Marshal Petain. The monastery had previously bought a nearby property called Farnborough Court and it was also transformed into a hospital which Eugenie added to her rounds.

If her political intervention over Dreyfus was controversial, in 1918 it was more significant. Learning the Allies regarded Alsace-Lorraine to be part of Germany she produced a letter written to her by the German Kaiser, William I in 1871. In it he admitted that the provinces had been annexed during the Franco-Prussian War purely for strategic reasons and not because their inhabitants were regarded as Germans. She forwarded the letter to the French Prime Minister, Georges Clemenceau via his dentist, Napoleon's "illegitimate son", Arthur Hugenschmidt, and it was enough to convince the Allies that the region must be returned to France, not bad for a 92 year old. She made one stipulation, the document must go into the National Archives as it was done for France not the French Government.

When the Treaty of Versailles was agreed, which formally ended the war, folklore suggested she took her copy of the special Times supplement and read out the clauses to Napoleon's tomb. Given her eyesight was so poor she could barely read the headlines I think it's a little far fetched but the romantics could imagine a word or two was spoken on her next visit to the crypt.

One piece of domestic wartime legislation really annoyed her. As a foreigner she fell under the restrictions of DORA, The Defence of the Realm Act so had to register with the Police and her movements were restricted to her immediate locale. Her car and petrol ration were given over to the hospital with no allowance for their extra needs but she refused to ask for a special dispensation. The act brought in a series of laws, designed to safeguard British security, some with severe penalties, amongst the lesser regulations was a ban on flying kites, having bonfires, buying binoculars, feeding wild animals and the introduction of new licensing laws including watering down alcoholic drinks (well perhaps that was serious). The whole idea was anathema to her and un English but she delighted in the victory over Germany, revenge as she saw it for Sedan. Her wartime efforts were justly recognised by a Honorary GBE, (Dame of the Grand Order of the British Empire), the Prince of Wales (Edward VIII) and the Duke of York (George VI) came down to Farnborough to present the award.

Her health had deteriorated during the war but not her spirit and she returned to Paris in December 1919 and then travelled on to Cap Martin. Ever the adventurer she wanted to fly but was dissuaded by everyone she consulted. She was desperate to have an operation to remove her cataracts but no English or French doctor would perform it since it normally required an anaesthetic, which came with risks for someone her age. However, her nephew, the Duke of Alba found a pioneering Spanish doctor who would operate without one and she set off in April. She sailed from Cap Martin, stopping off in Marseilles for an impromptu tour of the Pharo Palace, seeing it completed for the first time. As the boat passed Algeciras the British and Spanish ships fired a 21 gun salute in her honour, an unexpected but moving gesture.

She stayed with the Duke and his family and met up with her god daughter, Queen Ena. The operation in Madrid was a great success, she revelled in being able to read again and enjoy the Spanish sunshine, she even managed to relive her youth with a trip to a bullfight. On the eve of her departure, she suddenly fell ill and died a few hours later on July 11th 1920. She was 94.

Her body was brought back to Farnborough by train through France and huge crowds came out to pay their respects as the gun carriage progressed from the station to the Abbey.

The Funeral Procession through Farnborough July 18th 1920

The Irish guards formed a guard of honour and their band played the Marseillaise as no one could remember the Imperial anthem. Her coffin was covered by the Union flag which was replaced by an Imperial purple pall when placed on a catafalque in the nave.

The funeral two days later was attended by King George V, Queen Mary, the King and Queen of Spain and many other dignitaries. The French Government spitefully objected to the honours being paid to their former Empress so a planned gun salute was cancelled at the last minute.

Her mahogany coffin was placed in the Crypt awaiting the matching granite sarcophagus which now rests above and behind the altar.

Her estate was valued at around £2 million, much of it from overseas holdings (worth around £80 million in 2022). The house had been left to Prince Victor but there were many generous bequests to various

The Tomb of Empress Eugenie.

charities in England and France. He sold a variety of items over the next couple of years and his unexpected death in 1926 resulted in the sale of the estate and most of the contents to pay the death duties. Many of the artefacts, paintings, statuary and furniture were bought back indirectly by the French government and allocated to various museums.

The house was bought by the nuns who ran the local convent school and wanted bigger premises and is now an Independent Catholic Girls Secondary School. Their symbol is a Bee and their blazers, a Bonaparte green.

Plans to mark the centenary of her death in 2020 were cancelled due to the pandemic however a new bell was cast in her honour called "Eugenie".

Despite the criticisms levelled at Eugenie she remained remarkably loyal to France throughout, determined to salvage the reputation of the Second Empire. She steadfastly refused to have an official biography written to put her side of events but many unofficial memoirs and biographies appeared, a few quite critical and several written decades before were published on her death. By then most outside her diminished circle had lost sight of the Empire, washed away in the mists of time and her with it.

She is sadly neglected today and her reputation much maligned but she was a fascinating woman with an extraordinary life. Desmond Mountjoy, with his historian's hat on, regarded her as lacking in the intuitive gifts that make a good leader but with a great thirst for knowledge and personal courage "she had curious limitations but they were trivial compared to the great qualities she possessed".

Her friend of 30 years Ethel Smyth was certainly an admirer. "Whatever may be her faults they are of a noble character and one wonders how her worst enemies can ever have attributed littleness to her …her judgements are so temperate, so free from bitterness so generous and merciful".

Eugenie herself summed up her life as Empress "History said at the beginning I was a futile woman dealing only with clothes and towards the end of the Empire I became the fatal woman responsible for all the misfortunes. And the legend of history is always with the winner".

References and citations

Several museums have released parts of their archive as Open Access which allows free commercial use of their images and I'm very grateful to the Metropolitan Museum in New York and the Paris Museums group, especially the Musee Carnavalet whose collections I have drawn on. Those and other similar images are indicated as CC0 or PD (Public Domain)

The following are from the Library of Congress (LOC) Prints and Photographs division as referenced

P 11   Paris Panorama. LC-DIG-ppmsca-31565

P 24   Smithsonian. CC0 - via NPG gift of Mr and Mrs Dudley Emerson Lyons

P 70   Opening of Suez. LC-USZ62-95900

P 75   Surrender at Sedan. PGA - Schlegel--Surrender of Napoleon III

P 100   Eugenie. LC-B2- 1206-8

P 128   Sir Thomas Lipton. 1909. LCLC-B2- 911-12

P 142   Samuel Cody. Courtesy of Hampshire County Council. Provided by Hampshire Cultural Trust. Hampshire Record Office: HPP50/026

P 57,105,108,111,112, 147,148 © the author

Others not known but believed after research to be out of copyright.

Royal Archives
1 Diaries RA VIC/MAIN/QVJ (W) 4 Dec 1855 (Princess Beatrice's copy).
2 Diaries RA VIC/MAIN/QVJ (W) 10 Dec 1855 (Princess Beatrice's copy).
Other sources
British Newspaper Archive
Hampshire Archives
Royal Archives - Queen Victoria Diaries
Farnborough & Farnham Libraries Local History Sections

Bibliography – Principle books & articles

Bagpipe News April 2021 quoting Evening Telegraph of June 10-11, 1903

Bicknell, Anna. Life in the Tuileries in the Second Empire. Victorian voices.net

Carey, Agnes. Empress Eugenie in Exile. The Century Co. New York 1922

Chilot, Etienne. L'Ombre d'Eugenie. Le Charmoiset 2019

Chislehurst Society – several articles

Evans, Thomas. Memories. Vol 1 &2 Ed. Edward Crane (D Appleton & co 1905). Internet Archive

Famousdiamonds.tripod.com The French Crown Jewels.

Hegermann-Lindencrone, Lillie(**Moulton**) In courts of Memory. Urbana, Illinois. Project Gutenberg.Retrieved from www.Gutenberg.org/ebooks/7044

Hekmatist.com. Marx and Engels collected works. Letters 1852-55

Legge, Edward. The Empress Eugenie 1870-1910 via internet archive

Metternich, Princess Pauline. My Years in Paris. Forgotten Books

McQueen, Alison. Empress Eugenie and the Arts. Ashgate

Mostyn, Dorothy. The story of a house St. Michael's Abbey Press 1989

Mountjoy, Desmond. (D Chapman-Huston) The Melody of God. EP Dutton & Co 1922. Internet archive

Natalia.org.za . An Empress in Zululand.

Romer, John. History of the Valley of the Kings referenced in many articles.

Saunders, Edith. The Age of Worth. Longmans 1954.

Scott Polar Research Institute. Imperial hats blog Oct 6 2015 spri.com.ac.uk

Seward, Desmond. Eugenie, the Empress and her Empire. Sutton 2004

Sermoneta, Duchess of. Things Past. Hutchinson & Company 1929

Smith, William.The Empress Eugenie & Farnborough. Hampshire CC 2001

Smyth, Ethel Streaks of Life. Longmans, Green and Company, 1921

Thecourtjeweller.com 22.1.2015 - Empire's relics - NY Times Jan 21 1872.

Index